www.wadsworth.com

wadsworth.com is the World Wide Web site for
Wadsworth Publishing Company and is your direct
source to dozens of online resources.

At *wadsworth.com* you can find out about
supplements, demonstration software, and
student resources. You can also send e-mail to
many of our authors and preview new publications
and exciting new technologies.

wadsworth.com
Changing the way the world learns®

Managing Police Operations

Implementing the New York Crime Control Model—CompStat

Phyllis Parshall McDonald
Johns Hopkins University, Baltimore, Maryland

With contributions by Sheldon F. Greenberg
Foreword by William J. Bratton

WADSWORTH

THOMSON LEARNING

Australia • Canada • Mexico • Singapore • Spain • United Kingdom • United States

WADSWORTH

™

THOMSON LEARNING

Executive Editor, Criminal Justice: Sabra Horne
Developmental Editor: Terri Edwards
Assistant Editor: Dawn Mesa
Editorial Assistant: Lee McCracken
Marketing Manager: Jennifer Somerville
Marketing Assistant: Neena Chandra
Signing Representative: Jennifer Somerville
Project Manager, Editorial Production: Jerilyn Emori
Print/Media Buyer: Tandra Jorgensen
Technology Project Manager: Susan DeVanna

Permissions Editor: Robert Kauser
Production Service: Sara Dovre Wudali / Buuji, Inc.
Text Designer: Carolyn Deacy
Copy Editor: Robin Gold
Illustrator: Eunah Chang / Buuji, Inc.
Cover Designer: Ross Carron
Cover Image: PhotoDisc
Text and Cover Printer: Webcom, Ltd.
Compositor: Buuji, Inc.

Wadsworth/Thomson Learning
10 Davis Drive
Belmont, CA 94002-3098
USA

For more information about our
products, contact us:
Thomson Learning Academic Resource Center
1-800-423-0563
http://www.wadsworth.com

International Headquarters
Thomson Learning
International Division
290 Harbor Drive, 2nd Floor
Stamford, CT 06902-7477
USA

UK/Europe/Middle East/South Africa
Thomson Learning
Berkshire House
168-173 High Holborn
London WC1V 7AA
United Kingdom

Asia
Thomson Learning
60 Albert Street, #15-01
Albert Complex
Singapore 189969

Canada
Nelson Thomson Learning
1120 Birchmount Road
Toronto, Ontario M1K 5G4
Canada

Library of Congress Cataloging-in-Publication Data
McDonald, Phyllis P.
   Managing police operations : implementing the New York crime control
model—CompStat / by Phyllis Parshall McDonald ; with contributions by
Sheldon Greenberg and a
foreword by William J. Bratton.
      p. cm.
   Includes index.
   ISBN 0-534-53991-2 (alk. paper)
      1. Police administration—New York (State)—New Tork. 2. New York (N.Y.).
Police Dept. 3. Police administration—United States. I. Greenberg, Sheldon. II. Title.
HV8148.N5 M27 2001
363.2'068—dc21   2001026529

To my parents, Earl and Lena Parshall

My husband, Gerald McDonald

My children, Jennifer and Ray Novicio
Michael McDonald
Melanie and Jose Blanco

My grandchildren, Bethany, Jessica, and Amanda Blanco
Jesse, Hannah, and Zachariah Novicio

BRIEF CONTENTS

CONTENTS

I was very pleased when Phyllis McDonald asked me to write a foreword for this book on CompStat and the role it continues to play in the declining crime rates and improved quality of life in New York City.

The CompStat system and its results reflect a sea change in the way the New York Police Department does business. Like many large bureaucracies, the NYPD had been organized around avoiding risk and failure. For years, precinct commanders had been constrained on every side by regulations and procedures. Many police operations, such as prostitution sweeps and executing search warrants, could only be conducted by centralized units, reflecting an abiding distrust of precinct personnel and resources. Yet, despite all the micromanagement, the department was providing very little in the way of genuine strategic direction. It was clear what precinct commanders and personnel weren't allowed to do, but much less clear what they *ought* to be doing to combat crime, disorder, and fear.

Beginning in 1994, there were major changes in the management style of the NYPD. Precinct commanders were granted far more latitude in initiating their own operations and running their own shops. Uniformed patrol cops were authorized to make drug arrests and to assertively enforce quality of life laws, things they hadn't been doing for more than 20 years. At the same time, the central strategic direction of the department became far stronger and the lines of accountability far clearer. Avoiding failure is no longer a formula for success. Instead, the positive efforts of commanders and cops at reducing crime, disorder, and fear are being recognized and encouraged.

For the first time in its history, the NYPD is using crime statistics and regular meetings of key enforcement personnel to direct its enforcement efforts. In the past, crime statistics often lagged events by months and so did the sense of whether crime control initiatives had succeeded or failed. Now, there is a daily turn-around in the "CompStat" numbers, as the crime statistics are called, and NYPD commanders watch weekly crime trends with the same hawklike attention private corporations pay to profit and loss. Crime statistics have become the department's bottom line, the best indicator of how the police are doing, precinct-by-precinct and citywide.

At semiweekly "CompStat" meetings, the department's top executives meet in rotation with the precinct commanders and detective squad commanders from different areas of the city. These are tough, probing sessions that review current crime trends, plan tactics, and allocate resources. Commanders are called back to present their results at the "CompStat" meetings at least once every five weeks, creating a sense of immediate accountability that has energized the NYPD's widely scattered local commands. The meetings also provide the department's executive staff with an intimate way of gauging the performance of precinct commanders who have a better opportunity to be recognized for what they have accomplished in their commands and how effectively they are applying the NYPD's strategies.

Four steps or principles now guide the department's patrol and investigative work: timely, accurate intelligence; rapid deployment; effective tactics; and relentless follow up and assessment. Debriefing of people taken into custody, even for minor crimes, is now standard practice, greatly increasing the department's store of timely, on-the-ground intelligence. Computerized pin mapping and other contemporary crime analysis techniques serve as the NYPD's radar system, achieving the early identification of crime patterns. The barriers that long separated the department's Patrol Services Bureau, Detective Bureau and Organized Crime Control Bureau have been broken down, and a new spirit of cooperation is resulting in the rapid deployment of appropriate resources. Although overall strategy guidance flows *down* to the precincts, many of the tactics that are accomplishing the strategies flow *up* from precinct commanders, squad commanders, and rank and file police officers and detectives.

In the five-week "CompStat" cycle, the effectiveness of every new tactic or strategy is rapidly assessed. Failed tactics don't last long and successful tactics are quickly replicated in other precincts. The gathering of field intelligence, the adapting of tactics to changing field conditions, and the close review of field results is now a continued, daily process rather that an annual or biennial event. The NYPD can make fundamental changes in its tactical approach in a few weeks rather than a few years.

William J. Bratton

In November of 1989, after several years of experience at the managerial levels of police agencies, I joined the New York City Transit Police Department. I was the first female, and civilian, to enter top management of that department. I soon learned that morale of police officers was at an all-time low, and crime was at an all-time high. Ridership was declining seriously. The current police chief had come up through the ranks of the department and had already applied several innovations but was nearing retirement. In March of 1990, when he did retire, the Metropolitan Transportation Authority was gravely concerned and finally broke a 53-year tradition to hire a chief from outside either the Transit Police or the New York City Police Department (NYPD) to attempt to rescue the subways' serious decline.

I was not optimistic. I had worked for several chiefs and was aware that too often chiefs, and especially newly appointed chiefs, had to spend considerable time and energy on local politics, budget issues, and labor-management issues. Nonetheless, as the outsider was arriving at a decision about whether to take the position offered, I indicated to him that I saw great potential in this department of approximately 3800 sworn personnel. Since 1936, members of the Transit Police had attempted to overcome their status as "second-class citizens" in the City of New York, having to operate in the shadow of the NYPD, and had never succeeded. In the meantime, however, they had created excellent internal administrative systems, (discipline, training, and management information) in an effort to compete and "be the best." Also, this department was nearly corruption free. Still, patrol productivity was low, not effective given the rising crime rates, and officers needed new leadership.

The new chief made the decision to meet the department's challenges head on. I was completely unprepared for the individual who arrived on April 23, 1990. William Bratton had agreed to take the position on the condition that the Transit Authority officials accept the police as an institutional team member, unlike previous years where the police had operated in isolation, a serious disadvantage. He demanded the tools needed to "police," including a new radio system and an improved budget. He recognized the good things the department had accomplished.

He assured everyone that he would continue the Sector Team Policing effort, a version of problem solving and community policing partially tailored to transit policing. Within three weeks of his arrival, however, and after many long hours on the subway system with his police officers, he knew that a dramatically different approach was needed. The new chief was tireless, arriving underground on the subway tracks to speak with his officers at all hours of the day or night, never forgetting the details of a plan or program that was underway, and focusing on what his officers needed to increase productivity and perform effectively. In addition, he exhibited trust and confidence in his personnel, which resulted in new levels of creativity and eagerness to produce. Morale began to change for the better.

In late 1990 and early 1991, crime began to decrease dramatically in the City's subways. Ridership began to increase, and I began to realize that a new form of policing was evolving—one that was highly effective, efficient, and thorough. Yet, police leaders and theorists outside of New York were wary. They viewed the progress and techniques guardedly and quickly labeled them as being "outside of the mainstream of community policing."

This monograph describes the prototype of the New York Crime Control Model. It is also a "cook book" for implementing the model in other police departments for those chiefs and sheriffs who are searching for "a better way." Finally, this book is an effort to demonstrate that the crime control model is genuinely a means to strengthen and support the community policing strategy.

ACKNOWLEDGMENTS

I would like to thank several individuals who contributed significantly to this publication including Sheldon Greenberg, Chair, Interdisciplinary Programs, Johns Hopkins University, for editing this manuscript as well as writing the chapter on the relationship between CompStat and community policing, a most critical issue; Lt. Charles Pannell of the NYPD for providing samples of questions asked at the NY CompStat meetings; Superintendent Anne Marie Doherty of the Boston Police Department for providing copies of their innovative best practices document, CAMS; and Jerry Needle, Director of Management Studies of the International Association of Chiefs of Police (IACP) for his review and suggestions.

I would also like to recognize and applaud the efforts of the creator of the CompStat program, William J. Bratton, and his team of transit commanders, especially Michael F. O'Connor who succeeded William Bratton as chief of the Transit Police and continued developing the prototype of CompStat. And I would like to acknowledge the contributions of all those who worked to institutionalize the model in the NYPD: retired chief of the department, Louis Anemone; retired deputy chief of crime strategies, Jack Maple; former deputy commissioner of crime strategies, Edward Norris; and former commissioner of the NYPD, Howard Safir, who continued the program after Bratton's departure.

Finally, those police departments who were the first to replicate the CompStat process should be recognized. These police departments, in chronological order of replication are Boston, Massachusetts (Commissioner Paul Evans); Indianapolis, Indiana (Chief Donald Christ, retired); Baltimore, Maryland (Commissioner

Tom Frazier, retired); Prince George's County, Maryland (Chief John Farrell); and New Orleans, Louisiana (Superintendent Richard Pennington). Other major cities and agencies currently implementing CompStat are Broward County Sheriff's Department, Florida; Seattle, Washington; Austin, Texas; Los Angeles, California; Minneapolis, Minnesota; Lowell, Massachusetts; Longmont, Colorado; Mount Vernon, New York; Richmond, Virginia; the Maryland State Police; and the Royal Canadian Mounted Police, Canada.

Managing Police Operations

CHAPTER ONE

Historical Background of the NYC Crime Control Model

T he New York Police Department (NYPD) Crime Control Model, CompStat, is a vastly *new* approach to managing police operations and, as such, represents a "sea" change in law enforcement. This change is along two dimensions: First, this model represents a significant change in the management of police operations, perhaps the most significant in recent history. Second, the model represents a change in attitude toward the capacity of police to affect crime rates. The model is based on the principle that by controlling serious crime, police are better poised to maintain order and solve other community problems in the promotion of public safety.

Note: Throughout this book, the New York City Police Department will be referred to as the NYPD and the New York City Transit Police Department will be referred to as the Transit Police. The Crime Control Model was a program of the NYPD, based on a prototype developed by the Transit Police.

CHANGES IN POLICE OPERATIONS

CHANGES IN ATTITUDES TOWARD POLICE CAPACITIES

CHANGES IN POLICE OPERATIONS

Many police executives and researchers agree that traditional policing has been organized around the output goal of making arrests. Arrests are accomplished through

- Rapid response to calls for service
- Random patrol
- Reactive investigations

Mark Moore[1] expands the "three Rs" of policing and describes the police techniques used to accomplish arrests this way:

> *By patrolling public spaces and watching for criminal offenses; by responding to calls from citizens claiming that something that might be a crime has or is occurring; and, by investigating crimes that have occurred to determine who committed the offense, and to develop evidence against the offender that not only gives them the probable cause they need to make an arrest, but can also serve as the basis for a prosecutor being able to indict the offender for the crime and to win a conviction either at trial or in a plea bargain.*

The NYPD Crime Control Model represents a different view of police functions and operations than exists in many police departments. This book explains how the model evolved as well as how to implement it. The Crime Control Model story began with a new outlook toward police capacity and a recognition that police departments had been hampered for 30 years by negative beliefs about their potential to impact crime.

CHANGES IN ATTITUDES TOWARD POLICE CAPACITIES

In January 1996, *Time* magazine[2] posed a question that captures the current debate about the effectiveness of the police and offered a conciliatory conclusion: "Crime Rates Are Down Across the United States; Is This a Blip or a Trend?" Generally, the article concluded that current crime reduction is the result of both social changes and more effective policing strategies. More important, the author suggests that "It is respectable once again to believe that cops can have a real impact on crime rates . . . for decades they [students of crime] held that crime was too deeply connected to underlying social conditions . . . what changed is the [previously accepted] view that police are useful only to chase down bad guys after they strike."

Why did theorists in the past so thoroughly discount police capacity to impact crime? And how and why did that belief begin to change in the 1990s? These questions are important to understanding the NYPD Crime Control Model.

The 1967 President's Crime Commission report stimulated several key research efforts that resulted in raising serious questions about the effectiveness of the three

Rs of policing. "The Commission noted that there had been 'few scientifically controlled experiments' testing the deterrent effects of routine patrol."[3] Among the major research studies that followed were the Kansas City Patrol Experiment (1973) and the Newark Foot Patrol Experiment (1981), both conducted by George Kelling for the Police Foundation, and a study of the criminal investigation process conducted by Peter Greenwood for the Rand Corporation in 1975. The Kansas City Patrol Experiment, in its evaluation of the practice of random patrol, concluded that random patrol did not deter crime. Although the study focused only on one tactic, random patrol, the results were quickly interpreted to mean that no police patrol activities deterred crime. This overblown conclusion was no fault of the researchers, who should be applauded for having plowed new ground and opened the way to a new wave of research on police operations. The Newark Foot Patrol study concluded that foot patrol did not appear to affect crime occurrence but did reduce citizens' fear of crime. The Rand study of criminal investigations concluded that detectives solved crimes through witnesses and not through sophisticated investigative techniques.

As a result of these and other studies of police strategies, theorists quickly moved to serious and absolute conclusions regarding police effectiveness. Samuel Walker, for example, describes this syllogism:

> *There are serious limits to the crime control capacity of the police;*
> *Citizens play a major role in maintaining order in communities;* **therefore**
> *The police should direct their efforts towards strengthening the citizens' role.*[4]

He continues: "The police can and should direct more effort towards the less-serious problems of public order which set in motion the process for neighborhood deterioration—a process that culminates in high rates of serious crime."[5] This thinking is an apt description of the process that began to move police away from serious crime control and toward community policing.

These views dominated policing for two to three decades. Few people questioned these views, although there was some recognition that the major studies were limited in scope. Eventually, some began to realize that theorists had been flawed in their conclusions about the capacities of the police. It appeared that theorists had determined that (1) the way that the police functioned in the 1970s was the way they had always functioned and would continue to function, giving little recognition to any possible potential to change or improve; and (2) because the early studies showed that traditional police patrol had little impact on crime, and that traditional criminal investigations were not efficient, police could not, therefore, affect or control the occurrence of crime.

Theorists went on to explain that the reason the police could not impact crime was because crime resulted from social issues, such as poverty, drugs, and unemployment, although the cause-effect relationship was unclear. Police functioned using traditional enforcement methods of arrest, with the belief that although they could impact individual crime patterns through the arrest of an individual, for the most part they were handicapped in being able to change the general flow of crime.

In the mid-1980s the crack decade began, resulting in a dramatic increase in violent crime. Some began to speculate that although the police in and of themselves could not impact crime, perhaps with the help of the community, public safety could be achieved. Community policing was already being advocated, especially by those pursuing improved police community relationships. Herman Goldstein was criticizing the police and their methods but offering little about how his ideas would actually work in operation. He was astute in pointing out that police were overly concerned with management and efficiency and did not attend to the desired outcomes of policing.[6] The police are "reactive," devoting far too much time to answering calls for service and not enough to understanding the conditions and treatment that result in improvement. Most changes are fragmentary and do not represent a comprehensive plan. Goldstein criticized crime analysis as being applied too narrowly. Data should be gathered from a broader range of sources other than simply from police reports and should be used to understand the causes of problems and the impact of strategies. If the police were truly "problem-solving" it would, Goldstein suggested, push the police to think through how they respond to problems and to subject their responses to review of the highest authorities in the department. The bases for police decision making should be supported by data to reduce the likelihood of arbitrariness and faulty value judgments. Goldstein prophetically stated that skills, procedures, and research techniques to analyze problems and evaluate police effectiveness should be an integral, continuing part of management.

By the end of the 1990s, little progress had been made with either crime reduction or the spread of community policing, and even though some suggestions had been made about how the police could and should function, these ideas had not yielded a comprehensive plan of operation.

In 1990, officials in the NYC Transit Police, facing dire crime circumstances, decided to explore a new paradigm. This paradigm was experimental in that the Transit Police began to employ new approaches to police operations. Thus began a slow, evolutionary process by the Transit Police that led to unprecedented reductions in crime on the New York City subway system. This change occurred during a lull in national criticism of the police and external demands for change and at a time when the crack epidemic (starting in 1985) was leading to an increased demand for police protection. The Transit Police slowly realized that, contrary to expert opinion, the police could have an impact on crime: Well-organized and creative strategies coupled with high productivity altered the behavior of offenders, which resulted in far fewer victims. If perpetrators perceived that the police were "everywhere," they were less likely to commit their crimes, at least on the subways.

The model that began in the Transit Police was later applied in the Boston Police Department when William Bratton, with Jack Maple,[7] returned to that department for a short period of time. Bratton returned to New York in 1993 to become the Commissioner of the NYPD. He had successfully and dramatically reduced crime on the NYC subways[8] during his tenure as chief, and he was convinced that the model would reap positive results in any agency, regardless of size. Shortly, with reengineered police operations, crime began its dramatic decline across the whole of New York City. Initially, as with any experiment or radical change from the norm, some researchers and police leaders questioned the validity of the New York City results. Others began to consider that perhaps the police could significantly decrease crime, using the new data-driven accountability model. Still others denied that the NYPD experience could be replicated in departments outside New York City that did not have the resources of the 38,000-person force.

History would soon prove this view wrong.

SUMMARY

This book is intended to facilitate further experimentation with the NYPD Crime Control Model, to demonstrate that the police have greater capacity for reducing crime and improving the quality of life in communities, and to laud those police professionals who began to rely on the "collective police wisdom" and to achieve progress in the field of law enforcement.

I also seek to dispel some of the misinformation about the CompStat program to facilitate appropriate debate, experimentation, and implementation in state and local policing.

Notes

1. Moore, Mark. *The Police as an Agency of Municipal Government: Implications for Measuring Police Effectiveness.* Unpublished paper prepared for the National Institute of Justice, USDOJ, May 1996.

2. Lacayo, Richard. "Crime and Order," *Time,* January 15, 1996, page 48.

3. Walker, Samuel. *Between Two Worlds: The President's Crime Commission and the Police: 1967–1992—the 1967 President's Crime Commission Report—Its Impact 25 years Later.* Edited by John A. Conley, 1992. Cincinnati, OH: Anderson Publishing Company, page 30.

4. Ibid, page 31.

5. Ibid, page 31.

6. Goldstein, Herman. *Problem-Oriented Policing,* 1990. New York: McGraw-Hill, pages 14–49.

7. Jack Maple had been a lieutenant in the NYC Transit Police Department when Bratton arrived there in 1990. Maple became an advisor to Bratton in the Boston PD, 1992–1993, and joined Bratton in the NYPD in 1994 to become the Deputy Commissioner of Crime Strategies.

8. From 1990 to 1995, serious crime on the NYC subways was reduced by 75 percent. Ridership began its increase in 1993 as a result of the perception of increased security.

CHAPTER TWO

What Is CompStat or the NYPD Crime Control Model?

The New York Police Department (NYPD) Crime Control Model is referred to as "CompStat," or computer-driven crime statistics. CompStat is a multifaceted system used to manage police operations. In assessing the model and the New York City experience, some journalists and theorists have focused on only one or two components, which has resulted in a misperception and false assumptions about CompStat. For example, some have described CompStat as based solely on the pursuit of disorder, that is, a nuisance abatement or "zero tolerance." Others have described the Crime Control Model as aggressive policing, raising negative visions of the 1950s, police misuse of force, and violation of individual rights. Still others have focused on accountability and the unwavering demand that patrol commanders know and control the policing activities in their geographic areas of responsibility. This proliferation of singularly focused descriptors does a disservice to the management principles of CompStat and its potential for use in other jurisdictions. CompStat is a comprehensive, continuous analysis of results for improvement and achievement of prescribed outcomes.

NYPD CRIME CONTROL MODEL PRINCIPLES AND TECHNOLOGY
Specific Objectives
Accurate and Timely Intelligence
Effective Tactics

INVOLVING ALL LEVELS IN DESIGN OF STRATEGIES AND TACTICS
Rapid Deployment of Personnel and Resources
Relentless Follow-Up and Assessment
New Role of Executive-Level Commanders

NYPD CRIME CONTROL MODEL PRINCIPLES AND TECHNOLOGY

The implementation of CompStat, as set forth in the New York model, rests on five basic principles:

1. Specific objectives[1]
2. Timely and accurate intelligence
3. Effective strategies and tactics
4. Rapid deployment of personnel and resources
5. Relentless follow-up and assessment

Specific Objectives

Steven Covey[2] stated that all great people have one thing in common: They know what it is they want to achieve. This principle applies to law enforcement as well. The importance of setting specific objectives cannot be overstated. It is critical to the success of this program that the chief of police, in concert with top-level commanders, selects three to five crime-specific objectives for the year, or any reasonable period of time. This is important because establishing specific objectives sends a powerful message to all units: patrol, investigations, narcotics, canine, and others. This message indicates what the police department determines worthy of focus and attention. Examples of specific objectives are: decreasing street robberies, youth homicide, drug sales to juveniles, vandalism, car jackings, and many others. Objectives should not be expressed in percentages or numbers, for example, reduce robberies by 5 percent. Establishing an exact percentage of decrease can play itself out in several ways: Staff could react with immediate discouragement recalling earlier ineffectiveness in controlling crime; staff members could decide that once the 5 percent reduction is achieved they can rest and disregard the objective; or personnel might make every effort to achieve the numbers but without regard for appropriateness or long-term impact of the action—in other words, "we get what we measure." The wise police executive wants none of these reactions but, rather, wants to leave all possibilities open.

The police chief must be careful not to include administrative objectives in the list of objectives. Examples of administrative objectives might be installing one school resource officer in every high school or establishing 20 new DARE programs. Although administrative goals may be established in another context, they should not be interspersed with crime objectives for these reasons: Energies might become fragmented and dispersed; while developing a tactic or strategy to control crime, resources and efforts might be curtailed to meet the administrative objective; and often administrative objectives represent output measures rather than outcome measures. It is vitally important that all objectives be developed to represent outcomes rather than outputs. For example, an increase in the number of DARE officers or school resource officers may be reasonable, but ought to occur within the context of a total area strategy to reduce juvenile offenses and meet specific crime-reduction objectives. Ultimately, patrol commanders might decide that establishing a DARE program is one important tactic to decrease drug sales to juveniles, but it should be regarded as a long-term initiative. Otherwise patrol might become comfortable and nonactive with the attitude that no other tactics are needed because the DARE program will solve the problem. In reality, DARE might eventually contribute to the problem's solution, but should be considered a prevention strategy, not an intervention. Tactics and strategies development should focus on proactive and more immediate tactics that will achieve results faster, such as placing plain clothes operatives in the school to apprehend the drug seller who illegally enters the premises, or working with parole and probation to ensure that juvenile violators are returned to court for further action.

In the Transit Police Department in 1990, three objectives were established by the chief of police to guide all actions of the agency.[3] These objectives were "achievement or impact" statements, not "enabling or process" ones. Achievement or impact objectives define the desired outcomes of an activity, whereas enabling or processing objectives describe the tactics and strategies used to achieve the outcomes. The three objectives selected for the Transit Police represented the most serious problems facing the Transit Authority in 1990. Robbery, occurring at a rate of 30–40 per day in 1989, was considered the most serious. In addition to the reality of crime, fear of being confronted by an armed assailant in an isolated subway car or in the dark tunnels that characterized the subway gripped many passengers. Although the 30–40 incidents per day, among 3.5 million daily riders, represented a low probability of becoming a victim, concerns and behaviors of passengers were based on the perception of high probability. For some passengers, fear evoked by media coverage of a single violent event was sustained for a long period of time. Knowledge of a violent incident caused some passengers to seek other forms of transportation. The reputation of the subway system suffered. Thus, the first objective of the new program was the reduction of robberies.[4]

The second objective was eliminating disorder, largely caused by homeless people on the subway. Passengers traveling to and from work faced the possibility of entering a subway car or walking through a station and being confronted by a street person whose behavior was disruptive or caused fear. The behavior of some street people, which included urinating or defecating in the car or station, exacerbated the distress of passengers. The Transit Authority was acutely aware that this factor was deterring passengers from riding the subway.

The final objective was reducing incidents of fare evasion. Individuals jumping turnstiles or finding other ways to bilk the system were troubling to paying passengers and represented significant lost revenues to the Transit Authority. Although the illegal behavior of fare evaders was not threatening to passengers, it had two negative effects: First, it gave the appearance that there was no official or social control on the subway. Witnessing incidents of fare evasion fed the fears and discomfort of passengers and became a deterrent to subway use. Second, the drain of scarce financial resources inhibited repair and restoration of the subway system. The estimated loss per day to the Transit Authority was approximately $80,000 to 120,000.

The objectives set by the new chief were specific and firm: reduce robberies, disorder, and fare evasion. The chief of the Transit Police shared the three critical objectives using several different kinds of communication—videotapes, personal visits to districts and patrol officers on patrol, command staff meetings, and special meetings with sergeants, lieutenants, and specialized units. The Transit Police management team rallied around these objectives, and within a short period of time, sworn and civilian members of the department knew their roles in meeting them. District commanders were told that they could use their own discretion and creativity in managing their districts to accomplish the three objectives, but the objectives had to be met. District commanders were also told that they would be judged according to results.

In 1994, when William J. Bratton became the police commissioner of the NYPD, his approach to effecting change paralleled that used in the Transit Police Department. In his 1994 reengineering process, he used focus groups, interviews, and other techniques to assess the state of command of the NYPD. He then established seven objectives to provide direction to a fragmented organization of some 31,000 sworn members:

1. Get guns off the streets
2. Curb youth violence in the schools and on the streets
3. Drive drug dealers out of NYC
4. Break the cycle of domestic violence
5. Reclaim the public spaces of NYC
6. Reduce auto-related crime in NYC
7. Root out corruption and build organizational integrity in the NYPD[5]

These objectives were seen as a basis for reengineering the NYPD and the service it provided to its customers. CompStat was implemented to ensure that the objectives were met.

Accurate and Timely Intelligence

If the police are to respond effectively to crime and to criminal events, officers at all levels of the organization must have accurate knowledge of when particular types of crimes are occurring, how and where the crimes are being committed, and who the criminals are. The likelihood of an effective police response to crime increases proportionally as the accuracy of this criminal intelligence increases.[6]

Timely and accurate intelligence is the engine that now drives CompStat. Today, quality information and analysis provides the foundation for redirecting the energies of the NYPD.

In 1994, in the NYPD, crime data was available on a quarterly basis only.[7] Studying the Transit Police model, and committed to achieving the seven objectives, leaders in the NYPD recognized that improved, timely, and rapid analysis of crime information was essential to planned crime reduction. They began mapping incidents. Accurate and current crime data, when plotted on a map, provides a visible picture of problems across the city and within precincts. By comparing geographic (geo) maps over time, the data provided an overview of police response. When reviewed precinct by precinct, this data identified troubled locations, or "hot spots." When a hot spot remained visible for an extended period of time or crime incidents within a geographic area increased, it was an indicator that current methods of police response needed to change.

Soon after the comprehensive accumulation, analysis, and review of crime data began in the NYPD, operational changes began. Crime data allowed police executives to monitor hot spots and hold commanders accountable for their precincts. What is significant about the Crime Control Model is how all commanders, whether in patrol or specialized units, are held accountable. Top executives do not simply pass judgment on achievement but, rather, work with commanders to identify strategies and tactics that can be applied to a problem, and then together they analyze what did or did not work to achieve the desired results.

Crime data, combined with persistent challenge and support of leaders, produced results and led to the success of CompStat. In CompStat, crime data is reviewed to identify two types of situations: (1) troublesome or recurring hot spots, and (2) crime patterns. A geographic area, single address, street block, or area consisting of several blocks is deemed a "hot spot" whenever a series of criminal events occurs in that location. The crime events might be the same or might vary. In contrast, a "crime pattern" generally reflects the same crime event, often involving the same offender or group of offenders, but occurring in several locations rather than in a single location.

In the NYPD, technology is employed effectively for electronic pin mapping, which facilitates visual portrayal of both hot spots and crime patterns. As stated by Bratton, "Computer pin mapping and other contemporary crime analysis techniques are functioning as the NYPD's radar system, achieving early identification of crime patterns."[8] Examples of crime patterns are three gold-chain thefts on the "A Line" from Midtown Manhattan to the Bronx, a series of bank robberies across lower Manhattan, and a series of shootings in Brooklyn resulting in homicides and injuries. Examples of hot spots are a rash of burglaries in brownstones within a three-block area that occur following school closings, open air drug sales at a specific address resulting in assaults or citizens' complaints, and three purse snatches between 8 and 10 at night at the Wall Street Station in Manhattan.

Crime data used to identify hot spots and crime patterns can be derived from several sources. The most consistent, easily analyzed, and accessible is the traditional police management information system (MIS), which includes calls for service, arrests, and other police officer activities. The police MIS is a record-keeping system that collects and summarizes calls for service and reported activities. Many systems can capture response time to calls for service, time expended to handle a call, and reconciliation of the originating call category, for example, a robbery that is reclassified as a burglary after the officer completes the preliminary investigation. Time between the receipt of a call for service or reported police activity and availability of data for analysis can range from real time—that is, data is available as the event is occurring—to three months or more.

Other sources of data for analysis, though frequently more difficult to acquire for a crime analysis data bank or a geo mapping system, are the following:

- Information reported by the public through means other than 911
- Police officers' intelligence and field interrogation reports

- Information from other agencies, such as NYS Parole and Probation, U.S. Immigration and Naturalization Service (INS), or Federal Bureau of Investigation (FBI)
- Prisoner debriefings
- Informants
- Private security, for example, closed-circuit television (CCTV) and other observation techniques
- Police radios distributed to private security agents, citizen patrols, or auxiliary police[9]

Any police department using CompStat should derive data from as many sources as possible to ensure an accurate identification of hot spots and crime patterns.

Careful analysis and application of intelligence information has gradually led to changes in other police departments as well. When the Chicago Police officials began to focus on crime mapping and data it supplied, they realized that the beat officer alone could not solve all crime problems because many problems extended beyond the boundaries of the beat. Therefore, officials implemented a new strategy, similar to the CompStat process, to conduct meetings for strategy development on the basis of sectors and districts.

Effective Tactics

Effective tactics are prudently designed to bring about the desired result of crime reduction, and they are developed after studying and analyzing the information gleaned from our accurate and timely crime intelligence. In order to avoid merely displacing crime and quality of life problems, and in order to bring about permanent change, these tactics must be comprehensive, flexible, and adaptable to the shifting crime trends we identify and monitor.[10]

The second element of the Crime Control model consists of the strategies and tactics developed in response to an identified crime pattern or hot spot. CompStat has forced a new focus on how to create tactics and strategies that are both varied and highly effective. A conceptual example of the new strategy development evolution is displayed in Appendix A.

The Crime Control Model (CompStat) provides the impetus for creative and varied tactics and strategies. Most important, staff members with a variety of perspectives are gathered together regularly to examine problems and ensure that every idea and resource has been applied to developing a viable solution both at the command level and the precinct level.

Responsibility for exploration of resources and ideas rests with the chief of police or field operations commander. Having an executive at this level is essential to ensure that appropriate authority is present and capable of demanding cooperation by all operations and support units needed to address the hot spot or crime pattern. This individual ensures that all resources are considered in developing the most effective strategy or tactic for the particular problem. CompStat meetings provide the environment for developing a broad span of creative tactics and strategies to solve crime problems.

CompStat represents a significant change from the traditional model in which police leaders and units most often function independently from one another. In contrast, in the Crime Control Model, patrol is held accountable for crime in a given geographic area while investigations and all other specialized units are aligned to support the patrol activity. Specialized units that, in the past, functioned to achieve their own individual objectives are brought together in relationship to patrol. Support unit commanders are an integral part of the analysis process and are held accountable, along with their peers in patrol, for hot spots and crime patterns.

At regularly scheduled CompStat meetings, all units are represented. Commanders share information and responsibilities for successes and failures. Traditional inhibitors to cooperation—for example, time, distance, diverse objectives—are removed. Needs for cooperation are addressed "on the spot" at the CompStat meetings. Delays and excuses for not getting the job done are unacceptable and ultimately virtually eliminated. No one leaves the CompStat meeting until the tasks, and cooperation needed to accomplish them, are well-defined.

Reporting meetings are a centerpiece of a CompStat program. Requiring that precinct or district commanders appear before the designated police leader, whether the chief of police or an equally elevated staff member such as the commander of field operations, on a regular basis transmits important messages to the precinct commander and to the entire police department.

Some commanders might feel that because all units are assembled it would be a good time to attend to other departmental items. The chief of police and field operations commander must ensure that the agenda is a single-focus agenda: crime and public safety. Other business should be attended to at other meetings, not at the crime control meeting. A fragmented agenda could suggest that other items such as an upcoming recruit graduation are equally important to crime control. This should never be allowed to happen. An upcoming recruit graduation might be an important administrative item and should be addressed at a separate meeting devoted to administrative items. Mixing items tends to neutralize the importance of one over the other with the potential for managers to misunderstand priorities and misdirect subordinates.

As will be iterated throughout this book, traditional policing fosters independence of specialized units resulting in a silo-effect operation in a police department. Too often in the past, specialized units operated within a patrol jurisdiction unbeknownst to the patrol commander or any of his or her subordinates. When patrol commanders are recognized as being responsible for crime in their geographic areas and for needing to manage tactics and strategies that will amount to an attack on all crime problems, then they deserve the assistance of all specialized units that may be required for full solution to a problem. Crime control becomes much more creative and effective when patrol and detectives collaborate on strategy designs. Further, if a patrol commander decides, for example, that the only way to reduce street robberies in a four-block area during late night hours is to use a canine squad as a visible and threatening deterrent, then the patrol commander should have the absolute support of the chief or field operations commander to obtain the services of the Canine Unit. One of the more important functions of the chief or the field operations commander at the CompStat meeting is to have the capability of ordering or negotiating the services of specialized units for patrol commanders. The most critical factor here is that the crime control power of CompStat resides in the fact that all departmental units' activities are coordinated and integrated in support of the same objective. (See Appendix A, Organizational Location and Application of Support Units.)

The message should be that crime reduction is a priority and should be considered a serious endeavor of the police department, so serious that top leadership is willing to devote massive amounts of time in preparation for, and conduct of, the meetings. Personnel will begin to reorganize their time and energies to focus on crime control and reducing all crimes, harassing and disruptive minor crimes as well as serious crimes. Staff will be relieved when they discover they can now concern themselves with the critical work of a police department.

CompStat meetings should never be canceled or rescheduled, except for major natural or personal disasters. Although this edict may sound harsh, the reality is that staff members gauge the priority level of police agendas by the rates of cancellations or rescheduling of meetings. Once the meeting schedule is in place, it should be adhered to completely. It is equally important not to shortchange staff in the length of time devoted to the meeting. Whether one hour or even two hours are allotted, the executive-in-charge should make every effort to remain until all pertinent business is transacted. Cutting a meeting short because someone has another meeting is unacceptable. Police managers should realize that CompStat meetings consist of planning, assessing, and a rich exchange of ideas and information. These meetings represent the learning organization, and all in attendance stand to gain tremendously in their professional development.

Two basic issues are involved in holding commanders accountable: First is the process of convincing them that it is important to the progress and welfare of the police department and community that they assume responsibility for crime in their respective areas. Second, everyone involved must understand that there is a learning curve for this process and that commanders, previously held accountable primarily for personnel actions, must "learn" how to plan crime response strategies. Commanders must learn how to organize their own staffs, which resources are appropriate, how to work with specialized units, how to evaluate regularly to determine whether or not the desired results are achieved, and how to assess the creativity levels of their staff members to match suitable individuals with appropriate tasks.

When chiefs and other law enforcement executives begin to learn about the CompStat process, one of their first concerns is the ability to hold commanders accountable. The NYPD had the capacity to simply replace a precinct commander who was not performing with another. Most police agencies, however, have restricted numbers of members at the precinct or district commander rank level. Therefore, it becomes more of a challenge to hold them accountable because there is a limited supply of commanders for reassignment. Most chiefs viewing the earlier version of the NYPD CompStat process were concerned about publicly humiliating commanders as a way to motivate them to greater attention to detail. Psychologically, public humiliation, especially in front of subordinates, will result in retrenchment rather than motivation to perform. Chiefs have developed other alternatives and made observations that might help others in conducting a CompStat process:

- Holding one commander to task for a longer period of time during a CompStat meeting by asking an extensive number of probing questions to accelerate the learning curve and underline the criticality of the process

- Rewarding minimal successes, at first, as a positive reinforcer until the commander becomes more deeply involved in the process and energized by the satisfaction that comes with success

- Being stern and finding other behavioral ways to communicate displeasure with performance without verbally assaulting or insulting the commander

- Working with a commander's subordinates to get the job done, in the event that the commander exhibits reluctance initially to get involved (being bypassed tends to send an urgent message)

- Seeing that subordinates become invested in the process, with or without the commander, because this will motivate the commander to become involved as a way to reassert command and control

- Speaking in relatively harsh tones without demeaning the individual, addressing criticism directly to performance or behavior rather than to the personal qualities of the individual (this being the only way, for some personalities, to change the person's level of involvement)

- Demonstrating that the jurisdiction is receiving a lot of praise for its new actions to convince a commander that if he or she does not participate, promotion or other desirable positions will not be an option

For many departments today, as in the past, patrol commanders are held responsible primarily for personnel and administrative issues. The critical activity of crime control is either relegated to lieutenants or sergeants or, for some community policing departments, solely to the patrol beat officer (see Chapter Five). For the police department that is serious and truly concerned about public safety and crime rates, the patrol commander must be elevated to a central figure in the crime-control arena. An old police adage is this: What is counted is what is performed. In this case, the chief of police must focus on and reward the patrol commander for the ability to organize, create, implement, and execute strategies and tactics successfully. Ultimately, over time, the patrol commander position will become the status position within a police department. One factor that will help this process is that patrol commanders will acquire a new energy for their work because they will nearly always achieve success and because the process is an interesting and compelling one.

Some factions within a police department might have stern objections to the process. The detective whose self-image is supported by being perceived as a cut above patrol could experience fear and have strong objections to the CompStat program as he or she is asked to serve with patrol officers and assist them. The resistance might remain at a minimal level in front of peers, but it might be more severe in front of subordinates or outside the police department, such as with a mayor or city manager. The best situation is if the political structure of the jurisdiction supports the program. If the government leaders are not aware of or do not understand this program, there is a danger that the chief executive of the police department will waver in front of his or her immediate superior and subordinates, thus neutralizing the program. The chief executive, or other staff, conducting the meetings must stand firm. Any slight waver will be an indication that there is a way to defeat the program. If a field operations commander is conducting the CompStat meetings, it is important that the chief attend the meetings for a sufficient amount of time to communicate to all others that the commander of field operations has been given the authority to conduct the meetings and enforce decisions that have to be made. Further, the chief executive must determine whether any resistance to the program is the result of hidden or covert factors with the individual in charge at the next level down in the organization. All possible racial, gender, personality, and competency issues may need to be considered as possible sources of resistance.

The good news for this program is that most often—except for the notion that patrol officers should be in control, which can be troubling to some in a police agency—the nature of the work appeals to police and is most often translated as "this is what we should have been doing all along." The attendance of commanders of specialized units, investigations, and patrol at all meetings is critical to program success. Two major advantages accrue by having all stakeholders in attendance. First, the focal point for planning is a geographic area, so the interests and activities of all units become coordinated around a respective geographic area for greatest effectiveness. Integration, organization, and coordination are far more powerful in crime control than are fragmentation, disorganization, and random activities randomly applied. Second, agreements for services from units outside of patrol are negotiated in an organized manner and in front of the chief of police. As a result, strategies developed are synchronized between and among all units with a pertinent interest; negotiations are not conducted in a fragmented manner with specialized units that maintain the option of refusal to cooperate; and all participate in the design of tactics and strategies. The basic motivator should not be power but, rather, the achievement of an objective for public safety.

Many departmental resources can be called on in response to an issue. For example, NYPD officials, attending a training session, identified the following resources that a patrol commander could access to deal with a hot spot or crime pattern:

- Transportation-focused units, such as Traffic, Highway Patrol, Auto Crime, Motor Transport, Transit Bureau
- Community-focused units, such as Community Affairs, Homeless Outreach, Housing Bureau, Emergency Service Units
- Nonviolent crime units, such as Anti-Graffiti, Vandalism, Canine Apprehension Team, Crime Prevention Division
- Local and administrative units, such as Borough Task Force, Aviation/Harbor, Precinct detectives and specialty units, Police Cadets, Property Clerk
- Major crime units, such as Organized Crime, Narcotics, Anti-Crime, Crime Prevention Division
- Investigative units, such as TARU (Technical Assistance Response Unit), Patrol, SNEU, Investigation Division, Vice Enforcement, Legal Bureau

Resources external to the department were also identified. Representatives of any of the following agencies may be invited to attend CompStat meetings, especially when their resources may contribute to the needed solution:

District Attorney
Department of Motor Vehicles
Sanitation Department
Health Department
Buildings Department
Housing Authority/Housing and Urban Development
Department of Transportation
Sheriff
NYS Division of Parole
NYC Taxi and Limousine Commission
NYS Liquor Authority
U.S. Attorney
Secret Service
U.S. Postal Inspectors
Port Authority Police
Long Island Railroad Police
Area Police Private Police Liaison (APPL)

U.S. Parks Police
Board of Education
Environmental Protection
Fire Department
Department of Consumer Affairs
Parks Department
Department of Homeless Services
Department of General Services
U.S. Marshal
NYC Probation Department
NYS Police
Alcohol, Tobacco & Firearms (ATF)
U.S. Customs
FBI
U.S. Postal Police
Metro North Police
Immigration and Naturalization Service
Business Improvement Districts

Although the police exercise no control over these other agencies, making public safety the issue is likely to elicit a high level of cooperation. The administrator of the jurisdiction, for example, mayor or city manager, can also hold meetings, similar to the CompStat meetings held with police, in which he or she holds all agency heads accountable for both cooperation with each other and results.

A recent publication described CompStat as follows: "The key to effective tactics is focusing specific resources on specific problems. Random patrol most often produces random results."[11] This same publication provided the following list of specific tactics:

- Saturate an area with uniformed officers

- Saturate an area with plainclothes officers

- Set up checkpoints to find stolen cars

- Conduct narcotics "buy and bust" operations

- Conduct surveillance of an area with plainclothes officers/detectives

- Set up "sting" operations to catch fences who buy stolen property

- Conduct regular vertical patrols in buildings

- Use nuisance abatement laws to shut down illegal businesses

- Work with landlords to bring eviction proceedings against illegal businesses

- Do a warrant check on all persons arrested

- Have detailed enforcement plans in advance for problems likely to occur on specific holidays (e.g., patrols to prevent vandalism on Halloween, drunk-driving checkpoints on New Year's Eve), and make sure that the public knows about these plans in advance.[12]

Currently, most precinct commanders hold weekly strategy planning meetings. Patrol staff, specialized units, departmental legal representation, and other police or government units required for planning strategies to cope with identified problems are assembled to design plans. Precinct commanders use these meetings to prepare for the CompStat meetings, but the problem-solving focus has also become the way of "doing business" at these strategy-planning meetings.

INVOLVING ALL LEVELS IN DESIGN OF STRATEGIES AND TACTICS

Traditional police structure presumed that those in higher ranks were better able to make decisions and possessed greater creativity and wisdom than were line officers. The organizational development work of the 1970s and early 1980s by people such as Tom Peters and the community policing and problem-solving work of Robert Trojanowicz and Herman Goldstein sought to dispel this notion. These and other authorities espouse that all members of a department have the ability to be creative and should be involved in the decision-making process. Peters advocates that executives should "manage by walking around" and speaking with line staff. His rationale is that those on the front line possess as many creative ideas about how to improve processes and find solutions to problems as top-level managers do.[13]

The Crime Control Model operationalizes these management principles. Even though precinct commanders are held accountable for progress, members at all ranks and levels are expected to offer suggestions for solutions. Although managers must set clear objectives and know how officers in the manager's span of control are working to achieve them, ideas are garnered from all members. CompStat demands that communication occur throughout the police hierarchy, up and down. Officers' activities must be consistent with the objectives set by commanders. Officers and sergeants must accept responsibility for conveying problems and issues occurring in their beats. They must define solutions and convey results. Executive officers who do not communicate with or involve supervisors and officers will be unable to respond effectively to issues raised at CompStat meetings.

CompStat demands that communication occur across districts or precincts and units within the agency. An executive whose officers have concerns about obtaining information from the crime analysis or records unit or have problems with the fleet should address these issues with the appropriate unit commander before the CompStat meeting. Simply stated, CompStat holds all managers accountable for communicating, collecting and analyzing information, designing creative and varied tactics and strategies, and documenting results.

Precinct and district commanders are encouraged to bring whatever staff they deem important for the information-sharing process to regularly scheduled CompStat meetings. Commanders are encouraged to establish problem-solving teams in their precincts, districts, and units and to regularly draw on the knowledge and perceptions of sworn and civilian members at every level. Interunit problem-solving teams are sometimes established to review particular hot spots or patterns and suggest solutions. In the Transit Police, for example, four critical problem-solving teams were established: Robbery, Homeless, School and Youth problems, and Fare Evasion. These committees, which met biweekly, regularly generated new approaches to the issues under consideration.

The most important element in designing and selecting effective tactics is data collection and analysis. Without quality data and a commitment to conducting ongoing data analysis, the NYPD Crime Control Model will have less effect on reducing crime. Crime analysis dictates issues for discussion among police commanders and provides a framework for targeting resources to specific communities and crimes. The data provides the foundation for evaluating results as well.

Both the Transit Police and NYPD models showed that timeliness of data analysis is essential to success. If a CompStat command meeting is held weekly, new and updated data must be available weekly. If command meetings are held twice weekly, the data must be updated twice each week. Primary authority for directing the data analysis process rests with the chief of police or a trusted designee. Ideally, at the precinct and district level, data should be collected, analyzed, and distributed daily to all critical personnel so they can determine changes in criminal activity and direct the application of tactics and strategies and team problem-solving efforts.

Data analysis goes beyond simply tallying crime totals. It requires analysis by precise geographic area, methods of operation, and other trend indicators. Data analysis should consider factors such as changes in the number, demographics, or behavior of perpetrators; nature of arrests; adequacy of resources; and more. Analysis should occur whether crime remains static or increases. For example, the Transit Police analyzed the relationship between reduced fare evasion and arrests for more serious offenses. Fare evaders were being arrested for carrying weapons and other violations and checked for open warrants. Data showed that rigid enforcement of fare evasion quickly led to arrests of people carrying weapons and entering facilities to commit other crimes. In time, analysis showed that some offenders began paying the fare so they could enter the facilities to commit pickpocketing. The data analysis allowed the Transit Police to modify tactics as soon as new patterns of criminal activity began.

Quality data collection does not require multimillion-dollar computers or elaborate software packages, although automated systems are valuable. Quality data collection does require commitment and accurate information. Some agencies have done excellent jobs of analyzing data using index cards, legal pads, and calculators.

Rapid Deployment of Personnel and Resources

Once a tactical plan has been developed, an array of personnel and other necessary resources are promptly deployed. Although some tactical plans might involve only patrol personnel, for example, experience has proven that the most effective plans require that personnel from several units and enforcement functions work together to address the problem. A viable and comprehensive response to a crime or quality of life problem generally demands that patrol personnel, investigators and support personnel bring their expertise and resources to bear in a coordinated effort.[14]

One component of the Crime Control Model has received national attention and evoked considerable debate among police executives—CompStat command accountability. In the NYPD model, command accountability is deemed as important as data collection and analysis and the development and analysis of strategies and tactics.

Top officials in the NYPD know that the success of the Crime Control Model is based, in great part, on intense and consistent involvement of precinct commanders. Positive and negative behavior reinforcement are used in combination with role modeling to facilitate this involvement. Positive and negative behavior reinforcement are used based on the theory that praising or rewarding desired behavior and punishing negative behavior will lead to the type of behavior that is desired and extinguish that which is not. In CompStat, the desired command behavior includes investing time and interacting with other personnel to design solutions, using all available resources and subordinates to solve problems, and committing completely to crime control. Role modeling is also employed to affect precinct commander involvement. It is obvious at every CompStat meeting that the Chief of the Department and the Deputy Commissioner for Crime Control invest considerable time and energy toward reviewing crime data and generating creative ideas to solve problems. This point is never missed at CompStat meetings.

A critical reinforcer to involvement is holding command staff meetings frequently and regularly. At these meetings the Chief of the Department and the Deputy Commissioner for Crime Control, acting in concert, provide a model by asking a series of questions about specific crimes and precinct response strategies, crime patterns and data analysis, and specific goals. These officials demonstrate their knowledge of precinct-based data and crime trends because they invested time in reviewing reports and analyzing information before the CompStat command meetings. Until the precinct commanders become adept at generating strategies, the leaders suggest them. Commanders are then held accountable for implementing the agreed-upon strategies and are required to report on progress at the next CompStat meeting. At each meeting, copious notes are taken to record decisions, directions, and, most important, the follow-up to a problem that is expected. It is made clear to all which commanders will be called on at the next meeting to provide updates on progress.

The CompStat command meetings are a high-level learning experience. As precinct commanders of patrol, specialized units, and others in attendance observe the questioning, probing, and creativity, they are constantly learning how to reduce crime. Observers learn a range of tactics, how specialized units support patrol officers, and how impact and effectiveness are measured.

The leader of the CompStat command meeting—whether a chief of police, deputy chief, or other official—must be highly skilled, motivated, and committed to analyzing data and developing probing questions that will lead to meaningful results. The leader of a CompStat command process must ensure that a record of every issue and question is kept so that appropriate and "relentless" follow-up will occur. The CompStat leader must invest the time necessary to analyze problems, know every hot spot in the precinct under review, and be aware of crime patterns and trends. The knowledge and motivation of the people running the meeting is a driving force for other commanders. John Keegan describes this process as the "imperative of command": "The first and greatest imperative of command is to be present in person."[15] Although Keegan refers to generals during time of war, the principle applies to leaders in police service. By being present at every meeting, the leader of the CompStat process has his or her finger on the pulse of public safety activities. Leaders do not abrogate their responsibilities for analysis, tactical planning, or coordinating resources to solve specific problems. Rather, the leader poses informed questions and works directly with the commanders to solve problems and effect positive change. The leader is a teacher, reinforcer, and team member, not simply someone to whom others filter a report. As a result, an urgency to action is developed that ensures rapid response to problems. This rapid response begins to develop the impression that the police are effective and on top of community concerns. Perhaps the two most important questions the CompStat leader will ask at the succeeding meeting are these: Did you apply the solution that we designed, and what were the results? Probing for knowledge, information, and signs of constant and consistent attention to the problems and the process is the guarantor of success.

Relentless Follow-Up and Assessment

As in any problem-solving endeavor, an ongoing process of rigorous follow-up and assessment is absolutely essential to ensure that the desired results are actually being achieved. This evaluation component also permits us to assess the viability of particular tactical responses and to incorporate the knowledge we gain in our subsequent tactics development efforts. By knowing how well a particular tactic worked on a particular crime or quality of life problem, and by knowing which specific elements of the tactical response worked most effectively, we are better able to construct and implement effective responses for similar problems in the future. The follow-up and assessment process also permits us to re-deploy resources to meet newly identified challenges once a problem has abated.[16]

The final element of the CompStat Crime Control model is relentless follow-up and assessment. This is, perhaps, the most difficult element to sustain and yet clearly most important. Stephen Covey asserts: "We will soon break our resolutions if we don't regularly report our progress to somebody and get objective feedback on our performance. Accountability breeds response-ability."[17] The term *relentless* is an emotionally charged adjective that encapsulates several forces—determinism, doggedness, urgency, energy, and single-mindedness. These are all forces that improve performance by virtue of the fact that relentless or consistent follow-up increases alertness, productivity, and attention to detail.

Assessing and evaluating strategies and tactics is not common in police service. Yet, detailed and ongoing evaluation is critical to the continued success of the Crime Control Model. In the CompStat process, notes are recorded about every decision and change in tactic that will be used to achieve the desired results. Most often the precinct commander must return to the CompStat meeting the very next week to report on how he or she applied the newly designed tactic and to describe the results. If the desired results are not obtained, the process is repeated.

Methods of evaluation and variables may change based on the tactic or problem being assessed. All means should be employed to provide both qualitative and statistical assessment. Factors such as changes in crime patterns, continued existence of hot spots, continued citizen complaints, suspect identification, changes of patterns in calls-for-service, and arrests resulting in prosecutions, should be considered.

CompStat leaders should develop their own gauges of success based on quality research and analytical techniques.

Some suggestions for successfully conducting evaluation in the Crime Control Model are the following:

- Maintain detailed records of success and failures of individual tactics and strategies and then analyze them at regular time periods to determine which techniques led to success. Ultimately, this information can be accumulated so that certain techniques or tactics will emerge as being more effective than will others at solving a specific problem. These results are not only essential to the police department but also constitute critical learning to be shared with other departments engaged in a CompStat process.

- Acquire the services of an academic researcher to assist either by conducting the long-term trend analysis or short-term tactic-specific evaluations. This individual should attend CompStat meetings, observe, and provide suggestions to the staff on techniques that prove effective in evaluating individual tactics and strategies.

- Evaluate overall crime trends within a jurisdiction on an annual, semiannual, or monthly basis. This process is important for several reasons. It becomes the Department's report card to the community. The information can be used in budget processes for decision making on resource allocation and personnel distribution.

- Accumulate demographic and other data that might provide additional information explaining the dynamics of a crime trend. This process should be performed continuously to provide input to the CompStat process. It can be invaluable in understanding why a certain problem exists or is not yielding to suggested tactics.

New Role of Executive-Level Commanders

Former Deputy Commissioner of the Office of Management and Planning Michael Farrell, in discussing the changes that CompStat demands of the executive-level leadership describes the previous, traditional system that existed in the NYPD as follows: "A few members of the Office of Management Analysis and Planning would design a new tactic. All precincts would be expected to implement this tactic regardless of local circumstances."[18] By contrast, executive commanders must now begin by formulating a clear vision or mission regarding targeted objectives. They then must be prepared to "empower" the precinct commanders and allow them to develop allocation plans, tactics, and strategies to meet the objectives. Executives must encourage innovation and be prepared to accept the fact that not all new ideas will be successful. The new executive must move away from micromanagement and rigidity. He or she must encourage teamwork and include himself or herself as part of the team with the outlook that the team will succeed or fail together. Individuals will no longer be singled out and punished when a new idea is not successful. They must be prepared to examine failures and determine what went wrong and how the idea could be improved. The NYPD executive is prepared to organize and provide resources and address staff and equipment imbalances rapidly to facilitate action.

The NYPD executive also defines accountability. Accountability is not a vague or abstract term, leaving mid-level managers to wonder how they will fare at some final outcome. Accountability is exercised specifically and regularly as precinct commanders and others "account" for their actions to solve problems. The entire system of management requires a major, cultural change in an organization and infuses a sustained sense of urgency about solving crime problems and issues. The executive becomes the role model in that his or her primary concern consistently is solving crime problems and increasing public safety.

A recent NYPD publication recommends tasks that precinct commanders can use to follow up on their problem solving:

- Get out of their offices and drive around their precincts to see what conditions are really like.
- Review complaint reports of crimes daily.
- Review the precinct's "Unusual Occurrence Reports," prepared for shootings, rapes, and other serious crimes, daily.
- Review crime analysis materials prepared by precinct personnel (pin maps of crimes, reports of possible patterns, and other materials) frequently.
- Talk to uniformed lieutenants, sergeants, and police officers about crime conditions frequently.
- Talk to anticrime supervisors and police officers about crime frequently.
- Talk to the precinct detective and squad commander, supervisors, and detectives about crime conditions, and specific cases, frequently.
- Review precinct, borough, and citywide CompStat reports weekly, to see how the precinct is performing and to see how that performance compares to what other precincts are doing.[19]

SUMMARY

The NYPD Crime Control Model, CompStat, is a well-defined system for managing police operations. The model consists of a series of five steps that must be followed to achieve significant crime reduction. There are no limits to resources that can be applied to solve problems, and district or precinct commanders conduct their own precinct level problem-solving activities for greatest success. In this chapter, the behavior expected of the CompStat leader, most often the chief or deputy chief of field operations, is outlined.

Notes

1. I offset this factor and described it fully because it is such a significant part of the total process.

2. Covey, Stephen R. *Principle-Centered Leadership*, 1990. New York: Simon & Schuster, page 48.

3. *Action Plan—1990*. New York City Transit Police Department, internal working document, 1990, page 2.

4. The Metropolitan Transportation Authority, the parent company of the subway system, regularly conducted surveys of citizens in New York City

to determine attitudes and levels of fear regarding riding the subway.

5. Heskett, James L. *NYPD View: Harvard Business School Case Study for Class Discussion,* April 1996, page 6 (unpublished paper).

6. *The CompStat Process*, prepared by the Office of Management Analysis and Planning, NYPD, 1995, page 2.

7. Silverman, Eli B. "Mapping Change: How the New York City Police Department Re-engineered Itself to Drive Down Crime," *Law Enforcement News,* Vol. XXII, No. 457, John Jay College of Criminal Justice/CUNY, page 12.

8. Bratton, William J. *Great Expectations: How Higher Expectations for Police Departments can lead to a Decrease in Crime,* 1996 (December). Unpublished paper for the National Institute of Justice, USDOJ, page 13.

9. Executive Development Program, Course 324: *Crime Analysis for Strategy Development.* Unpublished curriculum, NYPD Office of Management Analysis and Planning, 1996, page 6.

10. *The CompStat Process*, prepared by the Office of Management Analysis and Planning, commanded by Deputy Commissioner Michael Farrell, page 2.

11. Guiliani, Rudolph, & Safir, Howard. *CompStat—Leadership in Action,* 1998 (May). New York: NYPD, page 5.

12. Ibid. page 5.

13. Peters, Thomas J., & Robert H. Waterman, Jr. *In Search of Excellence: Lessons from America's Best-Run Companies,* 1982. New York: Harper & Row, page 122.

14. *The CompStat Process,* prepared by the Office of Management Analysis and Planning, NYPD, 1995, page 2.

15. John Keegan. *The Mask of Command,* 1987. New York: Penguin Books, page 329.

16. *The CompStat Process*, prepared by the Office of Management Analysis and Planning, NYPD, 1995, page 2.

17. Covey, Stephen R. *Principle Centered Leadership,* 1990. New York: Simon and Schuster, page 49.

18. Farrell, Michael. Speech delivered at the U.S. Department of Justice, July 10, 1998.

19. Guiliani, Rudolph, & Safir, Howard. *CompStat—Leadership in Action*, 1998 (May). New York: NYPD, page 6.

CHAPTER THREE

Frequently Asked Questions About the Crime Control Model

This chapter answers some of the questions police chiefs most frequently ask about the New York Police Department Crime Control Model.

PLANNING FOR A CRIME CONTROL MODEL

What types of police departments should consider adopting this model?

This model has been used, thus far, in departments with 100 or more officers, though some agencies with fewer than 100 officers are experimenting with this program. State, county, and city police departments and sheriffs' departments are using the model. The operational principles of setting specific objectives, integrating and coordinating the functional units within the department, and using data for decision making apply to any department that is large enough to have separate functions. This model is frequently used in jurisdictions that have such severe crime problems that citizens are afraid to be on the streets. Fear by citizens may be the most salient criteria for selecting the crime control model, but any agency seeking to improve efficiency and strengthen the community should consider it.

What police departments other than the NYPD have implemented a crime control model?

The first department other than the NYPD to fully implement a crime control model was the Boston, Massachusetts, police department. Others soon followed: Indianapolis, Indiana; Baltimore, Maryland; Prince George's County, Maryland; New Orleans, Louisiana; Broward County, Florida; Washington, D.C.; Austin, Texas; Seattle, Washington; Mount Vernon, New York; Durham, North Carolina; Lowell, Massachusetts; Longmont, Colorado; Maryland State Police; Los Angeles, California; Chicago, Illinois; and San Diego, California. Most of these departments have experienced significant crime reduction, or at least report that they have improved control over crime, which they each attribute, in part, to the implementation of the crime control model. At a recent International Association of Chiefs of Police (IACP) conference, two thirds of all major cities indicated that they were replicating CompStat.

Would the crime control model work if it focused only on "crime problems" and not on specific precincts or area commands?

No. Focusing on a specific crime across a jurisdiction without affixing responsibility to an individual or group of staff responsible for a given geographic area negates accountability and dilutes effectiveness. When a patrol commander, representing a specific geographic area, is the center of focus, responsibility is fixed and some type of action has to occur. This is one of the most important elements of the crime control model. When a geographic area and its commanders are under review, problems are addressed as "hot spots" or crime patterns. The more narrow the area (e.g., one block, several streets) is, the better the analysis and the strategy can be. Holding an individual responsible for an area is the basis for accountability. Resources can be brought to bear on the hot spot or pattern. In contrast, talking about specific crimes in general terms or on a citywide or countywide basis rarely results in affixing responsibility to take corrective action, holds no one (or only one specialized unit) accountable, does not result in coordinated efforts, and achieves few significant results. In addition, when the focus is on a geographic area, several problems can be addressed simultaneously for improved efficiency.

Does a police department implementing the crime control model have to label it CompStat?

A police department implementing this model may be creative in deciding on a name. The Indianapolis Police Department labeled its program IMAP (Integrated Management of Patrol) and the Baltimore City Police Department has called its program CRIMESTAC, short for crime tracking and analysis.

What is the relationship between the CompStat Crime Control Model and community policing?

Generally, CompStat improves, complements, and supports community policing in a way not experienced before. Patrol commanders come to view community policing as another strategy to be used in crime control, and supervisors oversee and provide critical resources to community policing officers. (See Chapter 5 for a full discussion of this issue.)

Generally, how do communities react to this program?

Most communities react favorably to this program, particularly if the government leader of the jurisdiction and the police department explain the new approach accurately and understandably. Most often this program has been instituted in cities that have serious crime and disorder problems. As a result, when citizens see the increased activity, the new "smart policing" of their officers, they understand immediately that their department is demonstrating a heightened level of concern. This can result in increased involvement by the community to cooperate with the police. New York City has been the exception because recently there have been some heinous uses-of-force events. Many members of the community were quick to ascribe the issues to the CompStat program and the focus on serious crime. Research has not been conducted to determine the exact cause, but some believe that use of force is an ongoing occupational hazard for police because they always carry weapons. Others have considered the event "aberrations" that could occur in any department regardless of the management system. And still others see that one of the most serious events, which resulted in the death of an innocent immigrant, was the result of a "runaway" specialized unit that lacked sufficient training.

Do patrol officers tend to react favorably to this program?

Although there has been no formal research describing the reaction of patrol officers, most are at least neutral about the program at the outset. Some become enthusiastic for the wrong reasons. They hear the words "aggressive policing," initially associated with the NYPD program, and think that they are receiving permission to become abusive toward citizens. It is critical that the chief give the proper message. "Aggressive," as applied to a CompStat program, means higher productivity and renewed urgency. Some officers sense the new direction in the department, the new organization, and potential effectiveness and appreciate the change. They become great supporters of the program. Others realize that they will be allowed to use their professional knowledge to become more creative in designing solutions to problems that have the potential to receive far greater departmental support. Some sense that the role of patrol is, under the new program, the recipient of a new status and recognition, and as a result, they experience a new pride and interest in their work.

What can be anticipated by implementing the crime control model?

Within a short period of time, the following may be realized:

- Increased police productivity
- Improved information gathering pertaining to crimes and other community events
- Faster response to crime patterns
- Greater variety of tactics and strategies employed
- Better use of both internal and external resources
- Increase in the numbers of warrants served
- Increased gun seizures
- Targeted, rather than random, traffic enforcement
- Better-focused and better-quality arrests
- Increased field interrogations reports
- Improved preliminary investigations by patrol
- Improved intelligence gathering

    Other indirect results may include the following:

- Increased conversations about tactics and strategies among patrol officers and supervisors
- Increased flow of ideas from all rank levels
- Improved problem solving applied to community concerns

    Ultimately, the department can expect decreases in crime and increased public support.

IMPLEMENTING A CRIME CONTROL MODEL

How does a department implement a crime control model?

A staff member, of high rank who works directly with the chief of police, should be assigned to organize and coordinate CompStat meetings. This coordinator will make decisions about what data will be collected, analyzed, and provided to the chief and other high-ranking officials who participate in the meetings. The coordinator is responsible for scheduling and making sure that all appropriate persons receive the same data and are present at the meeting. At the meeting, the coordinator is responsible for keeping time and ensuring that appropriate notes are taken. Commanders may be initiated to CompStat by having them assist in setting overall objectives. In addition, training should be provided to all top-level staff. Information systems should be reviewed for adequacy.

How should police chiefs inform the department that the department is embarking on this program?

Various methods can be used. One department, for example, chose to take all top-ranking personnel to a retreat to discuss the program and their roles, to set specific crime-related objectives, and to select a name for the program. A chief could hold staff meetings with each rank level, offer a presentation, and then provide an opportunity to ask questions. Similarly, a chief could prepare a video announcing and describing the program (it is also very effective to continue to produce videos on experience and progress, as often as every two weeks, to keep department members informed about the CompStat process and other critical issues); special meetings could be held with staff whose work load and activities could change dramatically as a result of the new programs, such as crime analysts, geo mappers, and patrol commanders. As soon as possible, training should be prepared for entry-level recruits and in-service training provided for officers, sergeants, and civilians.

Do the city administrators need to know about this program, and is their support critical to success?

Crime control model plans should be shared with city administrators, and most chiefs have experienced positive reactions from the city administration when they have chosen to implement this program. In addition, having the support of the city administrators becomes important if either the community or police personnel have some objection to the plan. It is always important that the city administrator know and understand the major strategies employed by the police department. The city administrator becomes the conduit for information to the press, the city council, and the community. And, finally, as the police begin to include other city services in their crime reduction strategies, the city administrator must be prepared to support involvement by other city services to achieve police objectives.

How should the model be described to the press, community, government officials, and others?

The CompStat model has been labeled many things, most of which describe only one or two, or no, features of the program. It has been called a nuisance abatement program, an aggressive policing program, a zero tolerance program and a program to hold commanders accountable. All these labels fall far short of the model's true nature. Rather, CompStat should be considered enhanced leadership and management that focuses on a restructuring and integration of police operations driven by a scientific analysis of data. This model is a reconfiguration of the relationship between patrol, investigations, and all other specialized units that shifts departmental priorities from administration to crime control, especially by the chief of police and other high-ranking staff. In short, CompStat should be described as a system to manage police operations.

Will the financial cost of implementing CompStat be significant?

No. Generally, there are no increased expenditures in either manpower or resources. This program results in more efficient and effective use of both manpower and resources. If the implementing department is highly deficient in information technology, however, it will probably need to expend resources to acquire hardware and software. Ultimately, implementing the crime control model may reduce costs overall because of increased efficiency and effectiveness.

How many police officers will be needed to implement CompStat?

Unless the department is seriously understaffed, no additional officers are needed to implement CompStat. The essential factor in a CompStat program is the reorganization and restructuring of patrol, investigative, and specialized units for support and integration leading to greater efficiency.

DEALING WITH TRAINING AND PERSONNEL ISSUES

How will the crime control model change departmental job descriptions and what various personnel do every day?

The patrol commander's daily job will probably be far more intense, busy, and satisfying. The crime control model allows commanders to focus on public safety and problem solving rather than administrative paperwork. The more competent commanders will find themselves reaching out to others inside and outside the department for creative solutions to issues. The commander will have the opportunity to become a leader of substance to the precinct or district.

What types of training should be provided?

This program has the potential to affect the nature of performance of all personnel. Therefore, training should be delivered to all rank levels and civilians over time. The crime control model restructures and reorganizes police operations, so it is critical that managers receive training as soon as possible. This training should ensure that managers have a clear understanding of the objectives, purposes, and functions and have the skills needed to perform well within the program. First-line supervisors will require training in tactics execution, analysis of individual officer performance, and deployment to successfully implement specific tactics and strategies. Ultimately, new training components should be added to recruit and in-service training. These new components should include, at a minimum, skills in crime analysis and geo mapping, tactics and strategy design, implementation, and assessment.

The role of patrol commanders is vastly changed with the crime control model, so how should they implement the program?

The process is challenging. First, patrol commanders must ensure that crime data pertaining to the geographic area is regularly produced. A district or precinct crime analyst should be assigned to continuously review data to identify hot spots, crime patterns, and the impact of tactics and strategies employed to solve a problem. A complete briefing should be given to all personnel. Educating and motivating staff is essential. Community policing officers should support whatever tactics and strategies are employed in a given neighborhood. The patrol commander could establish a committee that spans ranks, assignments, and sectors to "problem solve" and develop new tactics and strategies. He or she should set up a system to track officer activities on an ongoing basis. The commander must visit trouble spots during all shifts, to gain a working knowledge of problem areas and to speak with staff about problems or patterns they are observing. The commander should be briefed every morning by the crime analyst, others in the command hierarchy, and any others critical to the process so the commander will be aware of all new hot spots and crime patterns. The commander should review activities employed the previous day to solve problems. In this daily meeting, calls for service should be analyzed.

What skills will patrol commanders need to use in implementing the crime control model?

The skills are somewhat self-evident: the ability to ensure that subordinates execute tactics and strategies as planned; the ability to understand and analyze crime data, hot spots, and patterns; the ability to involve subordinates in highly creative design of tactics and strategies; the ability to organize follow-up of planned activities; and the ability to assess the process, the outcomes, and the impact. The patrol commander will need to be able to communicate the nature of the program clearly and communicate expectations to subordinates. The commander must be prepared to negotiate activities such as increased traffic stops instituted to interrupt gun trafficking, for example, with the targeted communities. Some communities, if dealt with directly, will appreciate the increased activities that produce a safer community.

PROVIDING CRIME CONTROL INFORMATION

Is it important to share overall impact data with departmental personnel?

It is critical to share the impact with all staff, civilian and sworn alike. This progress becomes a source of pride and a motivator for increased action and attention to the problems. When progress is being made, many employees respond by increasing their efforts.

How often should crime data be made available?

Data must be available at least on a weekly basis. Daily availability, or "real time" (as each event occurs), is most preferred. Crime patterns change rapidly, and new ones can appear at any time, especially when the police are responding effectively. If commanders are to stay on top of changes, particularly changes wrought by their efforts, timely data must be available. Some large departments have technology and full-time crime analysts to supply crime data, progress, hot spot information, and crime patterns on a daily basis. But even in smaller and medium-sized departments, an employee can compile and analyze data manually working on a part-time basis. The key to success is to analyze often and analyze well. One department that did not have adequate technology selected a set of crimes that were primary to its objectives and had police officers in the field fax reports of the specific incidents to the person responsible for crime analysis.

Who should receive crime data and how frequently?

Dissemination of timely, accurate data is one of the keys to implementing the crime control model. When a police agency keeps employees aware of progress toward objectives, trends, and strategies, members are more likely to become motivated and interested, and energy levels and productivity tend to increase. Therefore, quality information must be shared with every departmental employee on a regular and ongoing basis. Essential to the crime control model is that all commanders be provided with crime data and analysis for their areas as frequently as possible. The data should be sent to all personnel, preferably daily, so that all departmental members become as aware of hot spots and crime patterns as is the patrol commander in whose area they operate. Patrol commanders should receive crime data every day for their areas. Only by reviewing all events within his or her area daily can the patrol commander effectively manage resources and ensure appropriate and rapid response to developing crime patterns. The patrol commanders must receive the same information as does the chief of police or the executive-in-charge of the meeting and at the same time intervals. Doing less inhibits the accountability process and sends a message to commanders that the process is not driven by data on actual activity within the community. Such a situation would only diminish the involvement and commitment of the commanders.

How should visuals, such as electronic pin mapping, be employed?

The importance of visuals cannot be overstated. Providing a clear picture of the area and trend data being discussed provides a common frame of reference that ultimately ensures understanding. If a department does not have electronic pin mapping or other devices, any conveyance to show data (flip charts, transparencies, chalk boards) can be used.

What format should be used to organize and report data at CompStat-style meetings?

Each department tailors the reporting form to suit its own needs. Generally police agencies compile the following data points, at a minimum, for analysis:

- A comparison of time periods: year-to-date, month-to-date, week-to-date, and previous day.
- A comparison of functional activities: crime by categories for each of these time periods, arrests for each major crime, summons issued, and cases closed by category.
- A comparison of geographic areas: by precinct or district and citywide.
- Crime maps that highlight a whole district or precinct by single type of crime and a smaller area, such as a two-block area with related crimes displayed.

Often data pertaining to the area patrol commander is included on the data sheet for the respective precinct or district including years of service, education level, previous major assignments, and possibly photos. Readers may want to contact individual CompStat departments for copies of data sheets to assist them in making decisions pertaining to data.

HOLDING COMPSTAT-STYLE MEETINGS

What are the purposes of the meeting?

Purposes of the meeting are the following:

- Ensure that patrol commanders are paying sufficient attention to crime in their geographical areas
- Ensure that the tactics and strategies designed to attack a problem are as creative and varied as possible
- Follow up on events from the previous meeting to demonstrate consistency and stay focused on crimes tied to the objectives
- Ensure that all departmental and external resources that could be brought to bear on a problem are coordinated and available
- Provide an ongoing teaching/learning situation in which those who attend can learn about developing strategies and assessing their impact
- Review the impact of tactics and strategies that are developed and applied

CompStat meetings are not general command staff sessions and should not include discussions of policies, budget, internal discipline, politics, organization structure, or any other item not directly related to crime reduction. CompStat meetings are not the place to discuss administrative matters.

Is confrontation with commanders a necessary component of crime control meetings?

No! The chief of police must have a clear strategy for communicating to commanders that they will be held accountable for crime in their precincts, areas, or districts and for the implementation of strategies discussed at CompStat-style meetings. Police commanders traditionally have not been held accountable for achieving outcomes, especially based on precise analysis of data, so some might attempt to cling to the status quo. This could necessitate their being challenged at meetings. If the "accountability message" is sent properly and commanders conform to analyzing data and planning and implementing strategies and tactics, confrontation will be unnecessary. In the NYPD, the first coordinators of the CompStat meetings were extraordinarily confrontational. Precinct commanders were humiliated and treated as if they were incompetent. Some speculate that this style was required to effect change in attitude and performance at that particular time. This harsh, confrontational approach to command meetings has become associated with CompStat—but wrongly so. In fact, this style is no longer employed by the NYPD. What is essential is that the police executive conducting the CompStat meeting communicates clearly that the department is committed to the crime control model and that poor or disinterested performance will not be accepted.

Which departmental members should attend the meetings?

The CompStat meeting is designed for the department's executive officers and those in primary decision-making positions (chief, deputy chief, bureau commanders, precinct or district commanders, unit commanders). Each session focuses on the activities in one or two geographic areas. Those commanders who are going to be involved in a discussion about trends and strategies in their districts may invite other members of their staffs who might play a role in, or add to, the discussion. Another group that should attend includes commanders from specialized units whose resources might be needed to adequately respond to crime patterns or other trends. Patrol commanders from adjacent areas or other patrol commanders who would benefit from exposure and experience may be directed to attend also.

Who should run the meetings?

In some departments, the chief of police has chosen to direct the meetings. This allows the chief to work with commanders and play a significant role in planning strategies. It also sends an important message to personnel about the value of the crime control model and crime reduction in the department. In some departments, the deputy or second-in-command conducts the meeting; in other departments, a commander, such as a deputy chief who has responsibility for field operations, conducts the meeting. The critical factor here is that whoever conducts the meeting must have sufficient authority to order the coordination of services (patrol and specialized units) to implement strategies. If the "field operations" commander is responsible only for patrol, the chief of police or second-in-command must be present to coordinate the work of specialized units.

Regardless of who conducts the meeting, the chief of police should attend often enough to remain up-to-date on progress, to provide quality control, and to emphasize the importance of the process.

Why is it important for the chief of police to attend the meetings?

The chief of police must send a clear message to personnel that he or she considers public safety and crime reduction the most important departmental concern and that all commanders, including the CEO, will devote valuable time to the meeting. Further, the chief of police cannot establish an accountability system for command staff if he or she is not going to play an active role. The chief sets the tone for the organization and for command responsibility.

What should the police chief's role be at the meetings?

Even if the chief of police is not conducting the meeting, he or she should feel free to ask questions of anyone in attendance. The chief should offer observations on the strategy, impact, and tactics. The chief should promote needed discussion about problems. The chief serves as leader, motivator, and, if needed, arbitrator. The chief should foster self-examination. The chief's purpose at the meeting is not to humiliate, threaten, or punish commanders. Rather, the chief should promote cooperation, collaboration, and partnering toward meeting crime control objectives.

Should community leaders and other members of the community attend CompStat meetings?

To date, no police agency has invited members of the community to participate routinely in CompStat meetings because most of the information should not be public. Some have invited the media to attend sessions for the purpose of publicizing a new program. Once the CompStat meeting format is well established, the potential exists to invite community leaders when the trend or strategy directly affects them. Representatives of federal agencies within the jurisdiction should be encouraged to attend. Representatives of local government units and prosecutors or district attorneys, whose cooperation and resources can be applied to a particular problem, should be encouraged to attend as well. The number of observers should be held to a minimum, however. The focus should be on candor and the work to be done, rather than on appearance, making impressions, or ensuring that some constituency is aware of action being taken.

How often should the meetings be held?

Meetings should be scheduled frequently so that patrol commanders recognize that the process is important and continuous. Frequent meetings are also important to enable the executive-in-charge to keep track of progress in each precinct or district in a meaningful way. Most departments conducting CompStat meetings require precinct or district commanders to appear at least once each month. To ensure that this schedule is maintained, some larger departments hold CompStat meetings twice weekly. Knowing that their precinct or area is going to be the focus of discussion frequently compels commanders to maintain their trend analysis and assessment of operational strategies. One reason that this model reduces crime is that an urgency is built within the police command that tends to increase productivity. This message is not lost on the perpetrators who begin to feel that the police are "everywhere all the time." This is an important message for the police to convey to enhance public safety.

What facilities or accommodations are required for the meetings?

The size of the room, auditorium, or command center should be sufficiently large to accommodate all needed presenters, staff, and observers. If possible, the meeting space should be equipped with overhead projectors, video production equipment, and computers to display crime data and geo maps. Adequate sound equipment to ensure that all in attendance hear all communication is essential. Also, all present must be able to see the data under discussion so they can understand and participate in discussions of strategies and tactics to combat identified problems. The use of LCD monitors and other devices designed to project computerized information keeps people focused and sharpens their awareness. Where equipment is not available, some departments have relied on printed copies of data.

What questions should the person conducting the meeting ask?

The regularly scheduled CompStat meetings have several purposes, so a variety of types of questions will be asked. The executive directing the meeting must ask precise, specific, and well-focused questions. He or she must avoid tangents and distractions and conduct the sessions so that all parties understand the expectations that evolve. It may be helpful for an assistant to observe communications between the executive-in-charge and his or her commanders to provide feedback to the executive-in-charge on issues such as how commanders responded to the interaction and whether or not pertinent staff appeared to be confused.

Generally, what are the reactions of commanders to these meetings?

When first implemented, some commanders are intimidated by the meetings. Several major changes to the traditional way of doing business are occurring simultaneously. First, the patrol commander is expected to focus his or her time and effort primarily on crime and the community, rather than on personnel or administrative issues, such as fleet, budget, or internal affairs cases, that traditionally consume the work day. Second, the patrol commander is expected to think creatively about solutions and allocation of resources to problems in his or her area. He or she is expected to draw on other departmental resources often off-limits to patrol commanders in the past. And, he or she is expected to report on trends, the problems facing an area, possible responses, and successes and failures for dealing with each hot spot or crime pattern. This occurs in front of peers, supervisors, and the chief of police. For commanders who have not been held accountable in this way, the model can be overwhelming. After a brief period of time, however, most patrol commanders respond well to the expectations and many become more involved in problem solving with their personnel than in the past. They also tend to find the process far more intriguing and satisfying than were the administrative tasks that had previously consumed them.

EVALUATING RESULTS OF THE CRIME CONTROL MODEL

How can police chiefs evaluate the success of this program?

The chief of police should recognize that three primary types of evaluations can be performed: process, outcome, and impact evaluations. In addition, the type of evaluation necessary for a CompStat program is an ongoing assessment of individual tactics and strategies. Process evaluations describe the operational factors of the program or department undergoing study to relate activities to outcomes or impact and to guide others in replicating the program. Output evaluations are essentially measures of productivity: number of arrests, number of warrants served, number of traffic stops, amount of drugs taken off the streets, or numbers of self-initiated activities by police officers. Impact evaluations are a study of the program's effects on the problem addressed: crime, fear of crime, and disorder. Assessment of tactics and strategies is an integral part of a crime control program and occurs as patrol commanders describe results of each tactic applied at the weekly meetings.

What measures should be used to determine effectiveness of the new crime control program?

Effectiveness measures are of two types and frequency:

- Long-term, cumulative comparisons of data, such as annual comparisons of serious crime or some crimes of serious concern to the community such as youth homicides. Comprehensive measures might include location and frequency of disorder complaints and measures of fear by citizens.

- Short-term assessments of tactics or strategies. For example, if a solution to a set of problems is being implemented, progress should be tracked carefully for the purpose of altering parts of the strategy. If, ultimately, the strategy fails totally, then a new approach needs to be designed and assessed.

Dr. Lawrence Sherman has prepared a provocative paper published by the Police Foundation in Washington, D.C., that discusses forms of measures particularly related to CompStat. The paper is entitled *Evidence Based Policing* and can be obtained by contacting the Police Foundation.

SUMMARY

This chapter answered major questions that police have about the crime control model, including

- Planning activities
- Implementation issues
- Training and personnel issues

- Data issues
- Details about CompStat-style meetings
- Evaluating results

Readers might want to arrange to attend a CompStat-style meeting in a jurisdiction with significant experience in the crime control model.

CHAPTER FOUR

Implementing a Crime Control Program

The letter "T" is set as a large drop cap for "This".

This chapter describes, step-by-step, how to implement the Crime Control Model, including suggestions for preparing the department to embark on a CompStat program. In addition, Appendix C contains two documents from the Boston Police Department: one, a copy of a staff document that is published at six-month intervals, lists tactics and strategies that have achieved desired results, and the other shows the department's format for presentations at their meetings.

PHASE ONE: PREPARATION

The following steps should prepare a police department to engage in a CompStat process.

Prepare the Command Staff

The process should not be undertaken without sufficiently preparing the command staff. One effective technique is to conduct a daylong retreat to discuss the purpose, rationale, technical elements, and anticipated changes in operations and job roles. Allow ample time for questions and airing of concerns. Either before or after the retreat, it is critical for all or some of the command staff to visit an active CompStat program. Generally, seeing a program in operation establishes the functions and purposes quickly and convinces commanders that the program is a sound one.

Involve the Jurisdiction Administrator

It is critical that the chief, either alone or with other members of the command staff, explain the program to the administrator of the jurisdiction. Allow a minimum of an hour or two for this meeting. The police department should ensure that the administrator understands the workings of the program, its rationale, and that it will not require additional human resources, but could require new staff assignments, such as centralized crime analysts. Be clear that the results are reduced crime rates achieved by a police service that is working "smarter" and that most CompStat programs have been received favorably by community members. The police chief might want to coordinate press coverage of the new program with the administrator of the jurisdiction.

Assess Departmental Systems and Facilities

Working with top commanders and knowledgeable technical staff, assess the capability of systems and facilities within the department that will be needed for a successful program. Assess systems for the following:

- *Ability to produce crime data in a timely and accurate fashion.* The management information system must be able to produce crime data in a timely and accurate fashion, preferably on a daily basis, but at least weekly.

- *Availability and accessibility of crime mapping.* Your command staff should evaluate the following issues: (1) Is there already a system in place? (2) Are technical staff members skilled in displaying crime data? (3) Is there the capability to display crime-mapping data on an overhead screen for large room visibility?

- *Availability of adequate meeting space.* Locate a room large enough to accommodate patrol commanders, commanders of specialized units, other command staff, other personnel as needed, representatives of other segments of the criminal justice system and government agencies as needed, and observers of the process. Ensure that the room has an adequate sound and visual projection systems.

At this point in the process two critical decisions must be made: Who in the department will conduct the meetings, and who will serve as the meeting coordinator? These two roles are critical to the overall success of the process.

The primary criteria for the meeting facilitator, the individual who will manage CompStat meetings, is sufficient rank to have authority over both patrol and specialized units. This position may be filled by the chief of police, especially in a smaller department, a deputy director of the department, or a field operations commander in departments where the field operations bureau or unit comprises patrol, investigations, and specialized units.

- The meeting coordinator must be capable of accomplishing a number of tasks for a CompStat process to be effective. The coordinator must schedule every meeting, notify relevant personnel, prepare the agenda, and check attendance. The coordinator must also ensure that crime data is accurate and available to all relevant staff in a timely manner and that the correct data for reports are available in advance of the meeting so that patrol commanders and the meeting facilitator have sufficient time to review the data. Another responsibility of the coordinator is making sure that crime analysts are present at these meetings and prepared to display data as requested throughout the meeting. In addition, the coordinator must supervise a recorder/note taker to ensure that the meeting highlights are documented, strategies and tactics are described, and an accurate record of points for the follow-up meeting are maintained. Finally, it is the coordinator's job to see that commanders who must return to the next meeting receive reminders and are listed on the agenda.

Establish Crime Reduction Objectives

To succeed, this program must have specific crime reduction objectives in place at the outset. Some chiefs have identified their objectives through a retreat with top-level commanders. Depending on the relationship with the department's labor organization, the chief might want to include leaders of the labor organization in the retreat process. At the end of this full- or half-day meeting, all should agree about the most serious crime problems in the jurisdiction that will have top priority in the CompStat program. Objectives should not be stated using percentages of crimes for reduction but, rather, should focus on the crimes to be reduced. Three other decisions should be made at this meeting: A name or acronym should be crafted that characterizes the specific program, preferably one that is unique to the department or jurisdiction; the staff should agree on a reporting format; and crime analysts should design samples of various designs for consideration. Finally, the chief or team needs to decide how frequently regular meetings will be held. Most chiefs implementing CompStat agree that the meetings must occur frequently enough that every patrol commander appears at least once a month or every five weeks. Having a longer period of time between regular reporting tends to diminish the importance and success of the program because there is insufficient time for an adequate level of detail. The NYPD, for example, found that to review the work of every precinct commander, meetings had to occur twice weekly with several commanders appearing at each meeting.

Prepare all Members of the Department

Another critical step is preparing the remainder of the police department personnel. A program announcement, with description and rationale, should be offered to every member of the department, civilian and sworn. The announcement should be as personal as department size allows. The program announcement can be made in a series of meetings to include all personnel in the department. Larger departments can prepare a video to be shown at all roll calls and in offices. Full explanations will ease tension and mitigate anxiety about the process. Taking time to fully inform all members will gain supporters who will be important for the success of the program. These meetings also allow the command staff to answer questions from those who either misunderstand or see the innovation as a personal threat.

PHASE TWO: IMPLEMENTATION

Meeting Rooms

The meeting room should be large enough to arrange one section for the meeting facilitator and other top-level commanders; one section with a podium for the reporting commander and relevant staff, and for commanders of specialized units as needed; and sufficient seating for observers, other related personnel, and representatives of other criminal justice and government agencies. The room should be able to accommodate a large video screen to display crime maps and other equipment for displaying related data. Two types of information will be displayed: crime data for the most important problem areas within the respective geographic area and electronic crime maps graphically displaying the area or subarea under discussion.

The NYPD has tables arranged in a hollow-square design with top-level commanders seated on one side of the square and the podium for reporting on the opposite side. Relevant staff members sit along the sides of the square while observers sit on rows of chairs behind the top-level commanders. The display screens are overhead at the opposite side of the room from the top-level commanders. Figure 4–1 depicts the NYPD room arrangement.

Meeting Procedures

The interaction at meetings should begin with the reporting patrol commander providing a summary of events and progress for the relevant time period and for the geographic area under his or her command. The patrol commander may ask commanders of specialized units who have been assisting with a particular problem to report their activities and results. Other personnel may be asked to contribute greater detail or review a tactic or strategy applied to a particular problem. The meeting facilitator should question the patrol commander at any time during the presentation so that information exchange is relevant and to the point. The meeting facilitator should focus on four topics: (1) a detailed description of problem areas, (2) the tactic or strategy that was used to solve a specific problem, (3) the results of the action, and (4) necessary follow-up.

If results are not as anticipated, the leader should check to determine whether the commander used all possible resources to attack the problem. The leader should check on the cooperation of specialized units, if they are not under the direct supervision of the patrol commander. The meeting facilitator may suggest other approaches, other resources, or other variations in a tactic or strategy that have previously worked well on similar problems. The meeting facilitator might, for example,

FIGURE 4–1 Room Arrangement CompStat Process

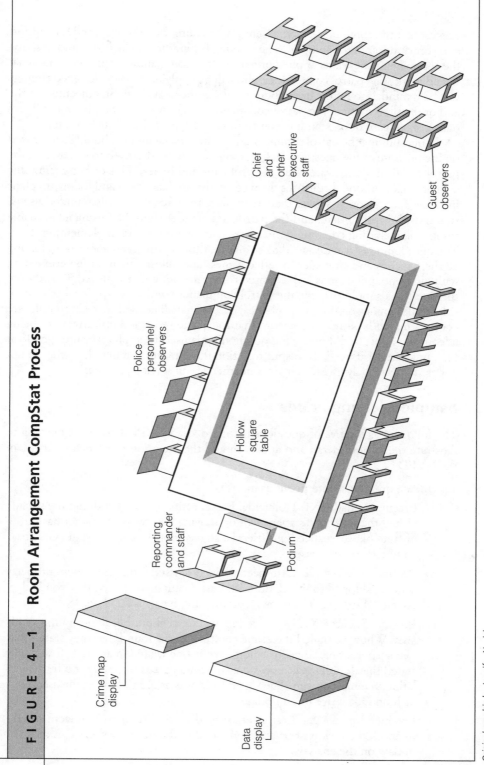

Crime map display

Data display

Reporting commander and staff

Podium

Police personnel/observers

Hollow square table

Chief and other executive staff

Guest observers

Original graphic by Jennifer Novicio

suggest that the community, media, schools, or churches be approached for support and contribution to the solution. The meeting facilitator may be direct and describe the action he or she wants applied or may ask the commander's opinion about what would work. The patrol commander who will be applying a newly designed strategy will be reminded to report back about results at the next CompStat meeting. At the end of the presentation, the patrol commander might want to compliment and recognize significant or outstanding contributions of specific individuals or units.

In questioning the patrol commander, the meeting facilitator should stay focused on the purpose of the questioning. Questions should be designed to ensure that the patrol commander is aware of all the problems and issues in his or her geographic area or neighborhood, prioritizes them correctly, and has action and follow-up plans in place. Tactics and strategies that are in place to attack the problem under discussion must be appropriate, and the patrol commander should be using all available resources, including community members and institutions, in implementing them. The questioning is also designed to ensure that the patrol commander is evaluating all these tactics and strategies for effectiveness and altering them or experimenting with different applications if the desired results are not being achieved. In addition, the questions should provide the patrol commander with new approaches to consider in designing solutions to problems, ensure that all needed specialized units are cooperating with patrol, and ensure that the crime reduction objectives are being adequately addressed. Finally, the questioning is used to apply pressure (gentle at first, but harsher if needed) to spur to action those patrol commanders who do not appear to be actively involved in or concerned about solving problems.

Sample Meeting Notes

The following is a series of questions recorded at an NYPD CompStat meeting to illustrate the level of detail and approach and the inclusion of agencies outside of the NYPD.

1. Update questions from previous meeting:
    a. Precinct Squad # X1: Homicide: Last meeting it was stated that the squad visited the girlfriend's apartment on moving day. Suspect's father has out-of-state plates; suspect's girlfriend also has roots to another state. Give us an update on this case.
    b. Precinct Squad # X2: Last meeting we discussed burglaries where property is being shipped to the Caribbean. Last meeting you stated that you had contacted the U.S. Customs Department. Give us an update.
    c. Precinct Squad # X3: Last meeting we talked about burglaries in the south area. When we pulled the crime complaints, we found that they stated that two suspects burglarized the home while one waited in an auto. It was stated that John Doe is a possible suspect and was stopped for a traffic violation in a maroon van. The squad C.O. was asked to look at the associates of John Doe. Give us an update.
    d. Precinct Squad # X4: Last meeting we discussed truancy. You were asked to check the recidivist truants compared to the burglaries. Give us an update on the analysis.

e. Robbery Squad: Last meeting we talked about a livery cab robbery pattern. Last meeting the squad commander stated that the case was to be closed shortly. Give us an update.

f. Precinct Squad X5: Last meeting you were asked to look into three sexual abuse cases. Give us an update.

2. Current day meeting questions:

a. Prior to questioning, the Borough Commander thanked two inspectors for their assistance in reducing the homicides and shootings resulting in a total crime decrease of 12%.

b. Primary issue—home invasions.

Question: Street Crime Unit: Do your people have anything to do with the home invasion arrests?

Answer: Yes. Three arrests. We arrested a suspect with a loaded 9MM, the second night out and two arrests one week later. These arrests occurred within the X precinct.

Question: Home Invasion Task Force: Two sting operations were conducted, one jointly with the FBI. Two cases were prosecuted federally. How are the suspects escaping from the house?

Answer: In both incidents they went to the rooftop out of the bathroom window.

c. Double Shooting: Squad commander gave background information on a double shooting including information on a suspect's welfare check situation and the fact that an HIDA[1] check was conducted. Check on second alias came back with an active warrant. Suspect has no driver's license. Since the suspect is on probation, we should have a lot of information about him in the system.

Question: What does his probation officer say?

Answer: Probation officer stated that the suspect never showed for his meeting, so a warrant was issued.

Question: Do we know why he was on public assistance?

Answer: No. Squad C.O. will check on this.

Question: Do we know who he contacted in his prior arrests?

Answer: No. C.O. to check.

Question: Was a Want Card dropped on him?

Answer: Yes.

d. Robbery: In discussing robberies, the C.O. stated that on one street, within a two-block area, there are five stores open 24 hours a day. He mentioned that within the same area there were two transit robberies and 2 cab robberies that resulted in arrests.

Question: Did we connect the cab robberies with any others?

Answer: No.

e. Domestic Violence Cases: Case one—Victim, who is common-law wife, was holding her four-month-old daughter when the suspect broke the victim's arm and hit her with a hatchet. A wanted poster was distributed. Information came back that suspect was staying with his first wife and may be in another state.

Question: Did we contact the other state?

Answer: Yes, they sent a photo of an individual with the same name that was not the wanted suspect.

Question: Does the suspect own a car?

Answer: No.

Question: Why don't we use a photo from February in the wanted poster?

Answer: We don't know if there was a photo from February.

f. Case two—After a review of this case, questions were asked about tours of narcotics team and the robbery squad.

g. Precinct Y: Review of homicide cases: Case one—C.O. believed that gunshot wound was self-inflicted.

Question: Were there any ballistics matching this case with the arson/homicide from another date?

Answer: There were no shell casings, and there is still no evidence that the victim in a previous homicide was shot.

h. In discussion of bank robberies:

Question: If the bank alarm goes off, what happens?

Answer: Two cars respond along with a supervisor. Everyone else will be directed to go elsewhere to cover highway exits and entrances. Bridge will be covered.

Question: Are you aware that there are cameras on the bridge?

Answer: Lt. Doe will contact DOT to monitor the cameras as well as to ensure that they are video taping.

i. In discussion of supermarket pattern: Suspect has been identified in five of the eight cases. Suspect was on lifetime parole and has been working as a maintenance man.

Question: Who did the suspect operate with? Who were his cellmates in prison?

Answer: The State Department of Corrections is being contacted.

j. Quality of Life Enforcement: After C.O. reviewed activities, question was asked.

Question: Will you report your activities and results back to the community?

Answer: Yes.

Question: Will there be follow-up?

Answer: Yes.

k. Information was presented on rape cases: Attempted rape, with a resultant photo hit; a search warrant was executed and property identified. Property sent to see if fingerprints could be lifted. We have a suspect identified.

Question: Why have we not shown photos?

Answer: We are searching for him.

Question: How many officers were out last night?

Answer: Four at various locations.

Question: Did he break his ankle when he jumped out of window?

Answer: No, he ran across the street.

Question: Were both sisters victims of the attempted rape?

Answer: No, he talked to one and followed the other into her apartment.

SUMMARY

This chapter provides specific guidelines to police agencies planning to implement a crime control program, including how to prepare all staff members to engage in CompStat-style meetings, why the jurisdiction administrator needs to be informed, the responsibilities of the meeting coordinator, how to identify program objectives, meeting room specifications, and procedural specifications.

Notes

1. HIDA stands for High Density Drug Analysis. These are regional programs funded by the Federal Office of Narcotics and Drug Control.

CHAPTER FIVE

The NYPD Crime Control Model and Community Policing

Sheldon Greenberg

Community policing is an organizational strategy based on the premise that the police and the community must work together to identify, set priorities for, and solve contemporary problems. Criminologist Mary Ann Wycoff defines community policing this way:

> The programs tend to have in common the belief that police and citizens should experience a larger number of nonthreatening, supportive interactions that should include efforts by police to:
>
> 1. Listen to citizens, including those who are neither victims nor perpetrators of crimes;
> 2. Take seriously citizens' definitions of their problems, even when the problems they define might differ from ones the police would identify for them;
> 3. Solve the problems that have been identified. . . .
> 4. Police and citizens should work together to solve problems.[1]

Some conjecture that community policing was conceptualized in response to the serious indictments against the police by the

SETTING A FOUNDATION FOR PARTNERSHIPS

DEMONSTRATING POLICE CONCERN ABOUT CRIME

COMMITTING TIME TO COMMUNITY POLICING

President's Commission on disorder, 1968.[2] Community policing was developed conceptually throughout the 1970s and applied in police departments in the 1980s by well-known police leaders: Lee Brown, Houston, Texas; Darrell Stephens, Newport News, Virginia; and Neil Behan, Baltimore County, Maryland. At times, the community policing concepts and requirements were combined with problem-oriented policing, an idea promoted by Herman Goldstein.[3]

Community policing, especially in relationship to the CompStat process, should be regarded as having three major elements. A police department engaged in community policing functions in a distinctive manner: The community policing department has an attitude of openness toward the community it serves, collaborates with its citizens to develop pubic safety, and cooperates with neighborhoods to marshal resources for problem solving.

There are no conceptual reasons to prevent community policing from being regarded as being totally compatible with CompStat. The CompStat system is a means to manage police operations and all police officers, whether they are engaged in community policing or other activities subject to management. Within the CompStat process, the activities, problem solving, and all work with the community by police officers is subject to the same reviews for effectiveness and efficiency as any other crime control activities are, and they are, similarly, provided with police resources to help solve neighborhood-level problems.

Therefore, community policing can—and should—become an integral part of any agency's CompStat program. The goal of community policing is to improve the quality of life and public safety in neighborhoods. Problem solving, public safety, and improved quality of life are the ultimate goals of CompStat.

Simply stated, CompStat demands that precinct and district commanders know their territories in the same manner that a patrol officer is required to know his or her beat or post. The crime control model requires that police managers view both problems and solutions within their respective geographic area as a whole piece of cloth, with a knowledge of how all the pieces fit together. This model requires that police managers integrate resources, internal and external, that they might not have used in the past. And, the crime control model requires that police leaders rely on quality information and analysis to keep abreast of problems and issues within their spheres of responsibility.

The concept of targeting time and resources and evaluating results based on careful analysis of data is part of the basic foundation of CompStat. It should also be part of the basic foundation of community policing. In addition, CompStat ensures that those officers assigned to be community policing (COP) officers will not function in isolation, are properly supervised, and are held accountable and that all strategies employed are integrated with other departmental strategies and that none are counter-productive.

The crime control model is not a contradiction to the "bottom-up" theory espoused in community policing. Rather, this model is where the "bottom-up" and "top-down" theories meet. In CompStat, a police manager must know how and where his or her personnel are functioning, the issues they are facing, their successes and failures, and their resource needs. The manager must anticipate issues of importance to the community—including serious crimes, lesser crimes, and fear levels—and, on an ongoing basis, assess progress in responding to these issues.

A chief of police in a large mid–Atlantic County department asked, "How can you hold police executives accountable for complex problem solving when they're not being held accountable for addressing serious offenses?" CompStat provides a level of accountability that has been missing in the community policing equation. In many agencies, the chief of police or sheriff who commits to community policing does so in the most professional and well-intentioned of ways. Officers and deputies are trained along with supervisors and managers and are directed to commit their time and energy to community policing as a way of doing business. Although the commitment of the chief executive and the mandate to field officers may be strong, measures of accountability at the upper-management and mid-management levels often are weak. CompStat provides the forum for upper-level and mid-level direction and accountability.[3]

The CompStat crime control model relies on comprehensive and timely data analysis to solve problems. The information shared at CompStat command meetings provides a base of knowledge to be shared with officers and civilian employees. CompStat requires quality data analysis and mapping that previously did not exist in many agencies—including many that embraced community policing.

Community policing and problem solving should be contingent on the use and analysis of data and assessment of strategies and tactics, and the CompStat crime control model already compels managers to apply these important criteria throughout all policing activities.

SETTING A FOUNDATION FOR PARTNERSHIPS

One significant lesson police have learned during the last quarter of the 20th century is the value of partnering and collaboration. Police experimented with, experienced, and ultimately accepted that they cannot control crime alone and in isolation and that they can be far more effective when working with the vast resources in a community. Several forces compelled police toward this approach. One critical force was the crack-cocaine epidemic that began in the United States in 1985 and changed the nature of violence and crime in communities. The police were overwhelmed initially and spent some time reorganizing their thinking, their resources, and their relationships with other law enforcement agencies and their communities. Simultaneously, some chiefs were pushing law enforcement toward community policing for other reasons as well. By the 1990s, partnering and collaboration had become a mode of operating throughout criminal justice and other segments of society. Police were not alone in evolving to this understanding. Other disciplines within the community began moving in the same direction—prosecutors, corrections, courts, public schools, social services, and the faith community. Finally, the conceptualization of community justice and restorative justice appeared. Together these forces not only changed the extent to which partnering was accepted but also led to many new experiments and progress.[4]

In early discussions of CompStat, some feared that brutality and excessive force were required operating stances. Others, particularly community policing advocates, rejected the system wholesale as being an anathema to community policing because accountability of patrol commanders could only mean brutal treatment and ulti-mately that brutality would work its way down the line to officers and citizens. As with any new concept or system, when there is a paucity of knowledge, the worst fears are resurrected and become the basis of opinion. As the dust has settled, however, more information has become available, many more departments are implementing this management system, and a more balanced and sensible view is spreading.

When properly implemented, the CompStat Crime Control Model becomes a positive link between the police and the public. This model draws public attention to the effectiveness of the police and, ultimately, becomes an indication to the com-munity that the police are genuinely concerned with public safety. When the pub-lic sees that police are finally being aggressive toward crime and focusing on serious crime, disorder, and the broad range of issues related to public safety, members of the public develop an attitude of cooperation and desire to support the police activ-ities—the New York City experience to the contrary.

CompStat is an accountability model that is applied to a myriad of undertakings by police and, in some departments, includes citizens' complaints and police viola-tions of rules and procedures. The crime control model lends itself to improving productivity and accountability in all units and is applied by commanders to the entire array of crime issues. The primary purpose of the model must, however, remain crime resolution through data analysis, accountability, strategy develop-ment, and implementation and assessment of tactics.

Like community policing, CompStat works best where there is beat integrity, but it also requires sector and district integrity. Integrity, here, means full knowl-edge of prescribed areas, responded to with carefully designed, effective tactics and strategies.

According to Thomas Frazier, former Commissioner of the Baltimore City Police Department, which implemented the crime control model in early 1997, this has resulted in positive changes in the way the police department does business and in no way inhibits community policing. Commissioner Frazier noted that, as a result of CRIMESTAC (Baltimore's name for the crime control model), all commanders know what is going on in the city and in their districts and units at a higher level of detail than at any previous time. Commanders can no longer ignore what is going on at the street level. They are compelled to demonstrate their awareness of crimes, trends, and issues in their districts. Similarly, Michael Butler, Chief of the Longmont, Colorado, police department, has stated that for the first time in his career, all his specialized units work in an integrated manner.[5]

The model adjusts the priorities of police commanders from administrative trivia to field operations, just as community policing adjusts the priorities of officers from responding to calls for service to problem solving with the community. "We must recognize the importance of patrol," Frazier continued, "We must become better at supporting patrol in addressing the needs of our neighborhoods. Arresting offenders—particularly violent offenders—is important to the public and is part of being a 'quality of life' agency and restoring neighborhoods in a meaningful and lasting way. The crime control model provides a way to turn attention to the impor-tance of patrol and community simultaneously."

DEMONSTRATING POLICE CONCERN ABOUT CRIME

In responding to a long-term public perception that serious crime was running rampant in a large city, a city council member remarked that the police department was seen as part of the problem. He stated that there could be only four reasons that police were not able to do more about how fear, crime, and perceptions of crime had gripped the city:

1. Members of the police department did not know how to investigate and resolve criminal activity.
2. Members of the department were afraid to get involved in matters related to serious crime.
3. Members of the police department stopped caring or never cared about the city and its crime problem.
4. Members of the department were corrupt, and serving their own aims took precedent over serving the public.

This police department implemented the CompStat crime control model and was able to demonstrate a new vigor in removing serious violent offenders from the streets and, with cooperation from the prosecutor's office, keeping violent offenders out of the community. In a relatively short period of time, the city council member began making positive statements about the police department. The chief of police noted, "If you do the big stuff, people perceive that the police department is doing its job—officers are not afraid, they care, they know how to do the job, and they're not corrupt." This is a clear example of a police department that refocused its priorities *and* organized itself to work "smarter."

A police agency that adheres to the philosophy and concepts of community policing and implements the CompStat crime control model will demonstrate its commitment to both crime resolution and community development and will experience far greater effectiveness in achieving its primary goal—public safety. Police executives and police officers will be able to say to citizens, "Trust us, work with us in partnership, see what we have done to better this community." This is a dramatic improvement over "Trust us, partner with us, look at what we hope to do."

According to retired Chief Neil Behan, Baltimore County Police Department, "Resolving serious crime is survival for most large jurisdictions. Getting a handle on serious offenses allows the department to do other things in conjunction with the community. There may be some jurisdictions in which solving serious offenses will not affect community fear, lead to resolution of other problems, or motivate citizens to partner with the police. However, most should realize a positive impact."[6]

COMMITTING TIME
TO COMMUNITY POLICING

One of the many myths about the crime control model is that time spent by officers in resolving crime will inhibit their ability to conduct community policing and problem-solving activities.

There is no basis for this concern. First, officers, supervisors, and commanders will be using their time more wisely. They learn to work smarter. And, they learn to work together. They target their energy based on ongoing crime analysis. This on-going analysis draws their attention to, and compels them to work on, serious problems in the community in conjunction with the less serious community problems. Productivity and success is judged on a regular basis based on quality analysis, targeted at precinct area and neighborhood crimes. Efforts and energies are not wasted because both focus on achieving important objectives. In addition, the crime control model requires that all personnel view the community as a whole piece of cloth and that there is an association between serious crime and behavioral and environmental disorder. When viewed in a comprehensive way, problem solutions emerge that are far more effective than a piece-meal, one-incident-at-a-time approach, dealing with incidents as though they were unrelated to other issues at adjacent or nearby locations. In this respect, CompStat puts the "community" in community policing.

Second, as officers focus on criminal activity in a comprehensive manner, other problems will be solved. For example, several officers were instructed to target thefts from autos occurring in their region (three adjoining beats). This was based on data analysis (presented at a CompStat meeting) that cited the method of operation, time pattern, and precise area of criminal activity. After three days of targeted patrol and surveillance, three suspects were arrested. A further review of crime analysis data showed a similar time pattern for serious vandalism committed to several public schools in the sector. One of the suspects confessed to the vandalism and implicated others. The officers met with school principals and security officers to ensure their willingness to prosecute. Ultimately, one of the suspects implicated in the school vandalism provided information on a person in the area possessing a stolen handgun. Patrol officers, in cooperation with criminal investigators and crime analysts, conducted the investigation in a specific geographic area. As a result of an initial focus on a single crime—auto theft—many problems were resolved creating a safer neighborhood.

Third, the public's willingness to partner in community policing activities can only be enhanced when the police demonstrate an aggressive and concerned approach to crime. Members of the public become energized as criminals are removed from the street and they see police targeting patrols in the neighborhoods of greatest need. In some communities, people will be more willing to attend meetings, participate in neighborhood patrols, share information, devote time to officers resolving problems, and so on when they feel safer and see the tide of crime changing for the better.

The model emphasizes the importance of partnering; initially units and commanders might have to be forced to cooperate if they have not done so in the past.

Precinct and district commanders no longer function in a vacuum but must work with peers and other units to implement strategies. Officers, supervisors, and executives see success resulting from internal partnerships among commanders and patrol and support units and can apply what they learn to beat-level community policing activities. In addition, the police partner works regularly and methodically with all government units, whether federal, state, or local, in solving problems. Finally, community assistance, a critical resource, is planned into the strategies.

Fourth, police officers will feel compelled and energized to get involved in more in-depth community problem solving when they realize they are having a positive effect on crime and when they see that the departments' command staff and supervisors are focused, working as a team, held accountable, and supporting officer-level efforts. When properly implemented, the crime control model brings together officers, supervisors, and commanders in patrol with all other specialized units.

SUMMARY

The CompStat crime control model does not preclude officers from becoming fully engaged in community policing. Within the CompStat structure community policing becomes more focused, efficient, and effective. While officers will apply a percentage of their time to high-crime or recurring-crime areas, as members of a multidisciplinary team, they will also identify and solve lower-level problems, partner with members of the community and organizations, engage other agencies of government and non-profit organizations within neighborhoods, serve the needs of special populations—all as part of a larger, directed strategy. More important, under CompStat the community policing officer knows that he can now draw on the resources of the department, that his or her commander is aware of the problems he or she is facing, and that these beat-level problems will be considered in the overall problem-solving plan for the district or precinct. At every level of the police department, from chief of police to patrol officer, CompStat reinforces the importance of using crime analysis, developing well-defined and tested strategies, and applying resources judiciously. CompStat ensures that police officers apply these same principles of sound and professional policing to community policing.

Many proponents have long espoused that there is a place for the "hard stuff" in community policing and that COP departments are less efficient if they ignore serious crime. An aggressive approach toward serious crime is as viable a component of community policing as creating and fostering new partnerships is. The CompStat crime control model forces a "seamless web"—a total efficient, effective, and scientifically derived police strategy whose basic goal is public safety.

> *"I know why there are so many people who love chopping wood. In this activity one sees results immediately."* Albert Einstein

Notes

1. Wycoff, Mary Ann. "The Benefits of Community Policing: Evidence and Conjecture," 1988. In *Community Policing: Rhetoric or Reality,* edited by Jack Greene and Stephen Mastrofski. New York: Praeger, page 105.

2. McDonald, Phyllis. "COP, CompStat, and the New Professionalism: Mutual Support or Counter Productivity," 2000. In *Critical Issues in Policing: Contemporary Readings,* 4th ed., edited by Roger Dunham and Geoffrey Alpert.

Prospects Heights, IL: Waveland, pages 255–277.

3. Goldstein, Herman. *Problem-Oriented Policing,* 1990. New York: McGraw-Hill, pages 14–17. These ideas first appeared in an article entitled, "Improving Policing: A Problem-Oriented Approach," *Crime and Delinquency,* 1979, Vol. 25, pages 236–258.

4. The reader should see the works of Barbara Boland, Todd Clear, and Katherine Coles and George Kelling for further information about these movements.

5. Frazier, Tom, and Butler, Michael. *CompStat for Small and Mid-Sized Cities.* Panel at the annual conference of the International Association of Chiefs of Police, Charlotte, North Carolina, October 31, 1999.

6. Behan, Neil. Unrecorded training session, Police Commanders Executive Development Program, the Johns Hopkins University, Fall, 1998.

CHAPTER SIX

Strategy and Tactics Development in Law Enforcement

INTRODUCTION

The advent of CompStat in the NYPD gave rise to a new focus on strategies and tactics that had been largely absent in law enforcement. Over the years the law enforcement profession has prided itself on being "para military." What was not recognized until the 1990s was that, law enforcement had borrowed heavily from the military in the form of promotions, ritual, rank levels, and uniforms but had not adopted the field of study of strategies and tactics. Even though strategies and tactics are the core of the military, this subject, before the 1990s, was not taught in police academies to either entry-level or in-service law enforcement personnel. Largely, this was because there was a unidimensional view of strategies and tactics in that patrol relied on a limited number of behaviors, as did criminal investigations and other specialized units (see Table 6-1 at the end of this chapter). In addition, the approach to crime control and public safety was one-dimensional in that crime problems were analyzed, if at all, one problem at a time as opposed to the CompStat notion of analyzing problems and issues by geographic units of analysis.

INTRODUCTION

CURRENT MAJOR STRATEGIES IN MODERN LAW ENFORCEMENT

Community Policing

Quality of Life

Quality-of-Life Policing and Neighborhood Economics

Zero Tolerance

Also, in the pre-CompStat days, strategies and tactics were selected to address one problem at a time, by functional area of the police. For example, the patrol function was generally confined to random patrol, response to calls for service, and close inspection of areas and was conducted only by patrol officers. Although criminal investigations used stakeouts, undercover operations, wire taps, warrant service, and other such tactics, only detectives used these tactics. Criminal investigators would address one issue, such as robbery, and analyze this issue across the city with the result that a single-dimensional strategy was designed for a single issue and used for all robberies across a jurisdiction. Patrol officers were occasionally used to accompany the service of a warrant, but for the most part, the patrol and criminal investigative functions worked separately and independently of each other and with their own distinct tactics, *even if both types of units were addressing the same problem within the same geographic area.* With the implementation of community policing, patrol began to branch out by incorporating community resources and those of other jurisdictional agencies and began to focus on minor, quality of life issues as identified by the community. Still, patrol officers operated in isolation from other functional units.

The CompStat process forced a new tactics and strategy paradigm in law enforcement. The CompStat process uses the geographic area as the unit of analysis and identifies all problems and issues within that single geographic area. Although the patrol commander is held ultimately accountable for problem resolution, all specialized units are expected, and held accountable, for assisting patrol. One significant outcome of this operating mode is that rather than a formula of one issue/one tactic, the result has been multiple problems and issues, multiple specialized units, and multiple tactics and strategies. For example, a plan for a geographic area riddled with drug pushers, unkempt and disorderly street conditions, and juveniles engaging in vandalism and harassing residents could include the following:

- A gang unit to emphasize that gang members' ability to be mobile could be curtailed if any are identified as trouble makers
- Officers working with parole and probation to identify and rid the area of any persons in violation of parole or probation
- Traffic enforcement to provide visibility of police, deter drug buyers, and reduce the number of guns in the area
- Cooperation with the public works department to clean up the streets and close or remove abandoned buildings
- Cooperation with the federal Immigration and Naturalization Services to remove illegal aliens
- Stakeouts, decoy operations, and surveillance by detectives
- Late-night street patrol by the canine unit

In other words, a comprehensive strategy comprising numerous tactics is employed to reduce and control a series of problems and issues, with a broad spectrum of specialized units cooperating in the operation.

To further enhance the effectiveness of the new strategy and tactic paradigm, continuous assessment is employed for two purposes: One, as a cybernetic, servo-mechanism,[1] or feedback loop, to detect need for small changes in the tactics, and, two, as a slightly longer term reading on whether all tactics employed within a geographic area are working to reduce crime and disorder.

Measures of success of a program for an area may include serious crime, disorder, and perhaps even surveys of residents to gauge levels of fear. When the progress of a set of tactics has stalled, the following questions should be asked:

- Has there been a reduction in police resources applied toward the specific problem?

- Has there been an overall increase in suspects intent on committing a particular type of crime? (For example, have a new group of immigrants arrived in the area, have drug dealers moved from an adjacent area?)

- Have the offenders altered their behavior to evade police action? (For example, have the drug dealers simply moved indoors?)

- Have the offenders moved to a new location? (This movement will become apparent as other geographical areas are analyzed.)

Thus, the CompStat process forces law enforcement to alter and adjust long-held, cherished beliefs about the nature of functional units, their separate and independent operations, their measures of success, and their level of creativity as applied to tactics and strategies—a true paradigm shift.

The following is an example of the array of tactics and strategies used to control crime on the NYC subway.

In the NYC subway system, serious crime was reduced significantly: Robbery by 80% over a five-year period (1990–1995) and all other crime by 72 percent during the same time period. Some simplified the Transit Police effort and deduced that crime was reduced because the police department focused its control efforts solely on fare evasion; the homeless problem; and, from 1984–1989, removing graffiti from subway cars. In other words, because considerable police activities focused on quality-of-life issues, the conclusion was drawn that crime was reduced solely because of the quality-of-life tactics. In fact, behind the scenes, and with less visibility, the Transit Police did far more than focus on the homeless and fare evasion. The Transit Police instituted an array of strategies and tactics directed at both serious and minor crimes[2] that completely changed the subway environment and sent a clear message to would-be suspects that if you target the subway, "the subway cops will get you." The Transit Police acted on the most critical principle set forth by Wilson and Kelling,[3] in "Broken Windows," an article that appeared in 1982 in *Atlantic Monthly* magazine. Wilson and Kelling maintained that, by instituting a series of tactics and strategies that effectively tracked offenders and interrupted crime patterns, a message that the system and community were "under control" would be transmitted to all people. Among its tactics and strategies, Transit Police took an aggressive approach to dealing with "wolf pack" robberies—committed by three to five juveniles. The Transit Police were no longer satisfied with arresting the primary robber but, rather, pursued the incident until all members of the pack were arrested. In addition, Transit detectives were assigned to the District Attorney's office to emphasize the importance of, and assist in the prosecution of, wolf-pack robberies. Another tactic employed by the Transit Police was to establish a system in which officers served warrants within three days after they were issued by the courts, rather than the six to eight weeks so often needed by other police agencies.

The warrants were often served at 2:00 A.M. for emphasis and to ensure that the offender would be at home. The Transit Police Central Robbery Squad had its offices in the basement of the building that housed the NY State Parole system. When offenders who had been arrested by the Transit Police returned from prison to visit their parole officers, they were immediately escorted to the Transit Robbery Unit. Detectives took their pictures and let them know that the Transit Police was aware of their return and would be keeping track of their activities.

A fourth tactic involved high-profile prevention of robberies of booth clerks. When robberies of booth clerks increased, detectives and patrol officers worked together to implement a deterrent program. The effort led to significant decreases in that form of robbery. The return of Transit Police decoy units was another tactic employed by the department. (Decoy units role play a victim to entice would-be perpetrators to attack the "victim," at which point the perpetrator is removed from the system, thus removing the threat from citizens.) In the late 1980s, the media had targeted decoys for criticism, and the tactic was temporarily disbanded but was re-instituted under Bratton for the purpose of patrolling for robbers and burglars before they could target passenger victims.

A new crime analysis unit was formed to track events on a daily basis. If a pattern (two to three crimes with similar offender descriptions or modes of operating) appeared, detectives and patrol officers cooperated to break that pattern. Most often this involved catching the offender in the act. It also involved providing targeted saturation patrols as a deterrent. The result of the energy, urgency, and activity devoted to this series of strategies was a message sent to passengers, potential offenders, and others that the system was "under control," and crime was significantly reduced.

From interviews with arrested offenders, it soon became evident that potential offenders had begun to view the Transit police as "robot cops" and ultimately advised others not to go on the subway to commit crimes. Over time and through analysis of crime patterns, the Transit Police realized that certain Transit Police activities could lead to a change in behavior by offenders. And even though the variety of tactics and unpredictability of when the police would appear led potential offenders to believe that the police were "everywhere," eventually the offenders figured out that they could change their own behavior as well. For example, as suspects realized that by evading paying the fare they were subject to being caught by the police, they began to pay their fares to go to other parts of the subway system to commit their crimes. In addition, suspects carrying weapons figured out that if they were jumping the turnstile to evade paying the fare, they should have their girlfriends carry their weapons, so that if apprehended they would simply get a citation for fare evasion rather than being arrested for carrying a weapon without proper authority.

In the near future, as law enforcement develops the specialized area of tactics and strategies further, trainers and strategists will begin to delve deeper into the subject by either working with the military to borrow the topics and references already developed or by studying the occurrences within policing, documenting and analyzing, and producing their own field of study. The study of tactics and strategies is not a new one; perhaps one of the first, and most widely studied, citations is an ancient history text produced in 4th century B.C. China.

Sun Tzu described "principles" of strategies and tactics in a book entitled *The Art of War*.[4] (Readers must bear in mind that Sun Tzu was a military general and, therefore, his language appears to be more aggressive than the modern strategist in law enforcement is comfortable with; nonetheless, it is important to realize that this subject applies to policing.)

> *The tactics and strategies of Sun Tzu place a high value on maneuver. . . . he adds that [the numbers of] indirect acts are as "inexhaustible as Heaven and Earth, as unending as the flow of rivers and streams . . ."*

In other words, there are few limits to creativity once unleashed.

> *All warfare is based on deception [unpredictability]. Attack him when he is unprepared appear where you are not expected.*

> *Do not repeat the tactics which have gained you one victory, but let your methods be regulated by the infinite variety of circumstances.*

> *Ponder and deliberate before you make a move. He will conquer who has learnt the artifice of deviation (variety). Such is the art of maneuvering.*

> *The general who thoroughly understands the advantages that accompany the variation of tactics knows how to handle his troops . . . So, the student of war who is unversed in the art of varying his plans . . . will fail to make the best use of his men.*

> *By altering his arrangements and changing his plans, he keeps the enemy without definite knowledge.*

Sun Tzu recognized that variety and unpredictability were important principles for success in battle. One important factor in crime control is creating the impression that the police are everywhere, always, and so adept that an offender could not possibly get away with committing a crime.

CURRENT MAJOR STRATEGIES IN MODERN LAW ENFORCEMENT

A number of other creations in modern law enforcement could, in some senses, be considered strategies but are often labeled "programs or philosophies." These must be considered in any discussion of CompStat policing strategies and tactics because they have generated considerable confusion among police practitioners trying to understand CompStat fully. Many of these concepts, such as community policing, quality of life, and zero tolerance, either have been not defined correctly or have been viewed as a panacea, for example, if a police department applied zero tolerance exclusively, all its public safety issues would be solved. The following discussion is an effort to clarify these misunderstandings and labels.

Community Policing

Many originators of the community policing concept were most eager to alter citizens' perception of the behavior of police from isolated, brusque, sometimes brutal but always aloof from the community to objective, open, professional, and fair and equal treatment of all encountered.[5] Early in the history of this movement, the description of community policing was that it was a "philosophy." Community policing could be considered a philosophy in that it required a departmentwide attitude change toward the treatment of citizens. Modern police departments recognize that their relationship with the community and individual neighborhoods will now never regress to conditions and practices of the 1950s. Police departments are aware that communities want to know crime data, often numbers of internal affairs cases and their resolutions, allocation plans of officers, and other information that is pertinent to public safety. Police can no longer function in secrecy. Modern police forces also understand the value of working with neighborhoods to marshal community resources in the service of public safety, to obtain much needed information about offenders, and to secure protection for police when faced with a crisis situation on the street. (The crime control successes in Boston are clearly the result of a multifaceted approach to public safety that includes the faith community, parole, probation, and the U.S. Attorney, all working in partnership with the police.) To this extent then, community policing can be considered both a strategy and an approach.

Quality of Life

At times quality of life is applied appropriately in law enforcement; other times it is severely distorted or misunderstood. The notion of quality of life derived from the Wilson and Kelling article discussed earlier. Wilson and Kelling describe what occurs relative to crime when there is a "perceived" lack of social control. Individuals perceive a lack or lessening of social control when any environmental or behavioral disorder is ignored, that is, when no one responds to clean it up or correct it, or where there is no corrective response to minor behavioral infractions. Social control, in this context, refers to all community, police, and other functions within a jurisdiction that operate to ensure adherence to a set of rules or expected public behavior. Unfortunately, there have been instances where this concept of social control has been misapplied to policing. In some communities, the assumption has been made that serious crime can be reduced *simply* by arresting large numbers of minor offenders. This conclusion has been reached because crime theorists have observed that serious crime is *associated* with disorder, both behavioral and environmental, but have not specified *how* they are associated.[6] The Transit Police has been widely cited inappropriately, through the clever misapplication of statistics, as having solved all crime problems on the subway simply through an overemphasis on fare evasion arrests. In some cases, this concept has been translated to mean that if minor crimes are "associated" with major crimes, then if the police arrest all individuals, across the board, displaying disorderly behavior, serious crime will automatically dissipate. It must be remembered that crime theorists confirmed that serious crime and disorder are associated but have not yet spelled out the cause-effect relationship. The reality might be that serious crime and disorder are on separate continuums and, although the two may occur in the same geographic area, further consideration is needed to understand the relationship exactly and to formulate strategies and tactics to combat both disorderly behavior and serious crimes. Human behavior is such that those who commit serious crime against society also tend to break minor societal rules. The *reverse* is not true, however; that is, all those who break minor rules do not commit serious crime. This behavior theorem complicates the application of the quality-of-life approach because if a police department attempts to arrest all minor offenders in an area, horrendous expenditure of police and court resources will exert an unreasonable drain on the jurisdiction with no assurance that serious crime will be reduced as a result. In addition, this approach has the potential to simply raise the ire of largely law abiding citizens, who, stopped at every turn for every little mistake, begin to feel harassed and still see the evidence of serious crime in their communities.

Police and sheriff's departments applying CompStat effectively use quality-of-life policing strategically. Offenders of minor offenses are arrested or stopped in increased numbers in areas of high crime, primarily in an effort to obtain information about serious offenders operating within an area. The expectation that by arresting all minor violators, crime will automatically decrease serious crime is misleading and simplistic.

Quality-of-Life Policing and Neighborhood Economics

When one defines disorder as both behavioral and environmental, new approaches to public safety emerge. Police are beginning to explore and understand the relationships between environmental disorder, crime, and economic stability. Early experimentation in Dallas, Texas, and Baltimore County, Maryland, shows that police intervention can prevent a declining neighborhood from deteriorating further. In the Baltimore County Police Department, crime analyst Phil Kantor[7] has shown that police resources targeted at a neighborhood facing economic decline (falling housing costs, drop in the number of small businesses, falling standardized school test scores, etc.) may prevent and turn the tide of erosion. He notes that, relative to the police department's ability to stabilize neighborhoods, police resources are better allocated to economically declining neighborhoods than to those that have deteriorated to an extremely low state and are characterized by high rates of serious crime. Kantor posits that it is more difficult for police activity to affect economic stability in these seriously deteriorated neighborhoods. Nonetheless, police realize that they will always focus significant resources in areas of greatest need based, in great part, on serious crime only and without concern for economic stability.

Former Chief Benny Click[8] of the Dallas, Texas, Police Department has devised an effective strategy that combines concern with neighborhood economic decline with community policing. His community policing officers approach an area by first identifying the significant stakeholders to economic viability, and then working with those stakeholders to develop strategies that will ensure their permanency, in conjunction with other community strategies employed, with great results.

The bottom line is that there is no easy answer to crime control. Simply applying quality-of-life policing will not eradicate serious crime. It is, however, critical for police strategists to understand the role of disorder, or quality-of-life policing, in relationship to all other strategies. Indeed, when disorder policing is combined with an array of other strategies, the police become that much more effective and powerful in their quest for both public safety and economic stability.

The NYPD is an excellent example of a police service that converted the notion of quality-of-life policing into a tactic and then incorporated it into a total strategy to combat crime.

The NYPD focuses on disorder arrests for two purposes. The first is to gather information about criminals. Those arrested for disorder crimes in a neighborhood are methodically questioned about more serious crimes such as weapons distribution to juveniles or individuals committing home invasions. Second, other strategies and tactics designed to maintain order are employed to bring neighborhoods under control. Once an area has been identified as being riddled with problems, several tactics are combined to bring about rapid change and create a sense of safety and well-being. Tactics employed in New York City, Baltimore, and other jurisdictions have included intensified warrant service, intensified traffic enforcement, enforcement of loitering and curfew laws, and working with parole officers to re-arrest any juveniles in violation of parole. In other word, tactics that would be labeled zero tolerance or quality of life are built into a larger strategy targeted at serious crime or a high crime geographic area.

The NYPD and Transit Police recognized that a multifaceted approach—setting clear objectives, reducing serious crime, focusing on order maintenance, long-term problem solving, and command accountability—was essential to success. Any singular approach might achieve rapid, short-term results but would not yield long-term and permanent effects.

CompStat has brought a new, unified approach to public safety. The new program quells the old debate about which are citizens more interested in— having the police focus efforts on serious crimes or nuisance violations. The NYPD and Transit Police both demonstrated that the two types of crimes are interrelated and that police tactics, strategies, and problem solving must also be interrelated for success. When a geographic area becomes the unit of analysis, all types of issues are attacked and resolved resulting in improved public safety.

Zero Tolerance

The zero tolerance concept has developed into a monstrous bugaboo for police, neighborhoods, and politicians. No policing effort is more severely misunderstood. Early in the development of CompStat, newspaper reporters used the simplistic term "zero tolerance" to describe a highly complex system of managing police operations. This term was quickly picked up by politicians, particularly those dissatisfied with their police, and, at times, by a "right wing" political contingency that was interested in returning to the old days when the police could be used by the majority to control the minority. The concept spread internationally, particularly to European communities who were experiencing a new rise in violent crime similar to that occurring in the United States.

"Zero tolerance," according to the misinformed means that the police arrest everyone for *every* type of offense in *every* type of neighborhood within a jurisdiction. One can readily see that to deploy police in this manner would rapidly reduce the effectiveness of the police. Mark Kleiman[9] hypothesizes that police effectiveness can be measured by the ratio of offenses to numbers of arrests, and when that ratio is in imbalance, potential offenders sense the imbalance and become more criminally active. Therefore, to deploy police equally without strategic considerations, ultimately will increase rather than reduce crime.

Frequently, the origin of the term was ascribed to then Police Commissioner, William Bratton, as driving the CompStat operation. When Bratton was confronted, however, he agreed that, indeed, he had used the term, but only as it applied to police rules and procedural violations, *not* to crime controls or strategies.

SUMMARY

Critical to understanding the paradigm shifts that revolve around tactics and strategies is viewing the entire array of changes that have occurred in law enforcement as it proceeded from traditional approaches of the 1950s and 1960s, to community policing (what I term "transitional"), to current operations management. Table 6-1, at the end of this chapter, summarizes the movements and perspectives of crime, disorder, and community satisfaction and illustrates both a continuity of movement and a gradual integration to produce a systematic approach to public safety.[10]

We must also recognize a new acceptance of a multidimensional approach to public safety. In a recent speech, Mark Moore,[11] Harvard University, attested, as a result of his years of studying policing and community policing, that police must approach public safety comprehensively, that one goal could not overshadow or subsume another. The three goals of public safety that the police must pursue simultaneously are control of serious crime, control of disorder, and fear levels of citizens. The CompStat approach to the police operations management illustrates the pursuit of a multiplicity of goals, a multiplicity of tactics and strategies, and an integration of police resources. This systematic and thorough approach, when pursued ardently and with serious effort and endeavor, will change law enforcement and create a new paradigm for policing in the 21st century. The actualization of a transformed and effective police service that functions with total integration and collaboration using all available resources is being implemented by departments across the nation. Research, study, experimentation, and dissemination are the necessary pieces to move the process from prototype to wide spread institutionalization.

Notes

1. The term *servomechanism* is defined by the *Encyclopedia Britannica* as an "automatic device used to correct the performance of a mechanism by means of an error-sensing feedback. The term *servomechanism* properly applies only to systems in which the feedback and error-correction signals control mechanical position or one of its derivatives such as velocity or acceleration. . . . Today, applications of servomechanisms include their use in automatic machine tools, satellite-tracking antennas, celestial-tracking systems on telescopes, automatic navigation systems and antiaircraft-gun control systems."

2. *Patrol Strategies Catalog,* New York City Transit Police Department, Michael F. O'Connor, Chief of Police, prepared by the Office of Management and Budget, Phyllis McDonald, Director, 1992.

3. Wilson, J. W., and George Kelling "Broken Windows," *Atlantic Magazine,* March, 1982, Vol. 249, No. 3, pages 29–38.

4. Philips, T. R. "Sun Tzu on the Art of War," *Roots of Strategy*. Harrisburg, PA: Stackpole Books, March 1985, pages 13–63.

5. The reader will remember that this movement in law enforcement was generated partly by the Civil Rights movement and partially by the President's Commission on Civil Disorder of 1968. The Commission's report represented a severe indictment of police and their relationships to ethnic communities.

6. Taylor, Ralph B. *Crime, Grime, Fear, and Decline: A Longitudinal Look,* 1999 (July). Research in Brief, Washington, D.C.: U.S. Department of Justice National Institute of Justice.

7. Phil Kantor is a crime analyst in the Baltimore County, Maryland, police department. He communicated these ideas in conversations with the author in the fall of 1997.

8. In conversations with author in 1997.

9. Kleinman, Mark, UCLA, in a speech for the National Institute of Justice, 1998, delivered for a *Perspectives* meeting in Washington, D.C. Videotape of this session is available through the National Institute of Justice National Criminal Justice Reference Service.

10. McDonald, Phyllis. Document produced for the Police Foundation, Washington, D.C., Brown Bag Presentation, September 1998.

11. Moore, Mark. Speech delivered at the Police Executive Research Forum (PERF) Annual Conference in San Francisco, California, April 1999.

TABLE 6-1   Perspectives on Crime, Disorder, and Community Satisfaction

Traditional

Unit of Analysis	Entire jurisdiction
Mission/Objective	General—Protect life and property
Data Analyzed	Selective or none; reaction to calls for service
	Serious crime more likely to be counted but not analyzed
Police Response	
Strategies/Tactics	Patrol: Random; response to calls for service;
	Specialized units: By type of crime; selective responses to incidents
Resources	Police only
Engine	Intuition, political complaints, calls for service
Accountability	Rules, policies and procedures violations
	Patrol: Response time to calls for service
	Specialized units: Productivity (arrests, amount of drugs removed from street, etc.)
Beliefs About Police	Police cannot impact crime/public safety or behavior of would-be perpetrator
Results	Bifurcated department; no impact analysis

Transitional

Unit of Analysis	Patrol: Beat area
	Specialized Units: entire jurisdiction
Mission/Objective	Patrol: interact with community
	Specialized units: protect life and property, occasionally reduce certain categories of serious crime, e.g., residential burglaries
Data Analyzed	Patrol: Beat area problems and issues via police data and neighborhood input;
	Specialized units: serious crimes (primarily counting with some analysis of hot spots/crime patterns by type of crime)

TABLE 6-1	Continued

Police Response	
Strategies/Tactics	Patrol: work with neighborhood to solve problems
	Specialized units: Self directed/selective problem solving; strategy/tactic by type of crime across entire jurisdiction
Resources	Patrol: Officer, community and government
	Specialized units: police resources of individual unit; at times, other police agencies
Engine	Patrol: Beat/citizens complaints; Crime data by beat area
	Specialized units: types of crime
Accountability	Violations of rules, policies, procedures;
	Patrol: officer response to neighborhood;
	Specialized units: productivity
Beliefs About Police	Police can have no effect on crime but can develop good community relations
Results	Bifurcated department; no impact analysis

Current/Developing

Unit of Analysis	Circumscribed geographic area-district, precinct, public service area/minimum—several beat areas
Mission/Objective	Control of serious crimes and the most troublesome issues impeding public safety
Data Analyzed	All police related events that threaten public safety (traffic, robberies, youth issues, parole/probation violations, auto theft, etc.) centralized and public service area, analysis of crime patterns and hot spots
Police Response	
Strategies/Tactics	An array of tactics and strategies to ensure public safety; coordination of all specialized units by geographic area commander; coordinated problem-solving-police and relevant government services
Resources	Police, government, community, other police agencies
Engine	All relevant and available crime data; complaints, calls for service; continuous centralized and geographic area crime analysis and crime mapping
Accountability	Geographic area commander; specialized units are decentralized and under control of the area commander and/or held accountable by high ranking official (This system is not abusive or punitive but leads to the "learning organization"); measured against stated objectives
Beliefs About Police	Comprehensive police strategy by unit of analysis provides message that area is under control; police can impact public safety, crime, and behavior of would-be offenders
Results	Integrated and "learning" police agency, collaborating with community, government, other police agencies; driven by specific objectives

(continued)

TABLE 6 - 1   Continued

Future/Potential

Unit of Analysis	Circumscribed geographic area as above, managed by a public service area manager
Mission/Objectives	To ensure public safety and community viability by public service area; each public service area has its own objectives to direct operations and hold staff accountable
Data Analyzed	All of crime and public safety data, plus economic and social issues data, e.g., domestic violence, school issues; and data on community court, corrections, and prosecution
Government Response	Combination of tactics and strategies that involve police, all criminal justice, schools, economic development, social service agencies
Engine	All crime data; all community data; social service agencies, all government agencies; community problem analysis
Accountability	Community service area manager and subordinates by jurisdictionwide management board who are experts in solving neighborhood problems, equalizing services, analyzing meta and micro issues, to ensure healthy, safe, productive community; e.g., the learning village
Beliefs	That collaboration/partnerships driven by scientific data analysis leads to comprehensive development of public service areas that are safe and viable
Results	Totally integrated public service area using all available resources and integrated strategies and tactics; driven by specific objectives that lead to ultimate community safety and viability

The Long-Term Significance of the NYPD Crime Control Model to the Development of Law Enforcement

CAUSES OF POLICING CHANGES

Most people recognize that change is inevitable, whether they accept it or not. Even though much rhetoric characterizes police agencies as being unable to change, many of the nation's large and mid-sized departments have changed significantly during the past 30 years. Change is provoked by internal and external forces or through positive and negative forces. In police agencies, change can result from legislation, public criticism, appointment of a new chief or director, or a mandate from a mayor or governor. Change can occur as the result of new technology, unusual social, economic, or political events, or litigation.

Despite all these influences, however, the most effective change occurs as a result of evolution. Evolution is change brought about through experience, legitimate need, scientific experiment, and collective wisdom. Evolution is often difficult to detect because it occurs slowly and proceeds, necessarily, one step at a time. In the 20th century, American policing proceeded through two major reform movements, both initiated by external criticism. In the 1930s and 1940s communities began to realize that their police were riddled by corruption, much of it low level and pertaining to hiring and firing. Citizens became so vocal that a President's Commission was organized to study the problem. In the late 1960s, two more President's Commissions were appointed to review both the police and the broader issue of civil disorder.

Police service is now in the midst of a third significant reform. This one is not occurring as a result of external criticism but, most significantly, because of "collective police wisdom."

External Criticism

From the 1930s to the 1960s, law enforcement slowly altered some procedures as the result of accusations of rampant corruption. This corruption, it was recognized, had been fostered by political control and interference in police department processes and yielded to civil service regulations for police. This period of change is regarded as a "Reform Era" for law enforcement and was shaped by many who are still regarded as great leaders in modern police service. Innovators such as William Parker (Los Angeles) and O. W. Wilson (Kansas City and Chicago), Patrick Murphy (New York and Washington, D.C.), Donald Pommerleau (Baltimore City), and others conceptualized and implemented the police professional model, including a focus on higher education requirements, improved entry-level and in-service training, and written policies and procedures.

Law enforcement began a second major reform period in the late 1960s and 1970s. This change was sparked largely by the President's Commission on Disorder (1968). The Commission's report was a scathing indictment of police. Among its primary recommendations, the Commission urged law enforcement to repair its relationships with minority populations and other special interests groups and to "humanize" the behavior of police officers. The police response to this indictment was the conceptualization of community policing. Community policing is the legacy of the second reform movement. Chiefs and leaders, such as Lee Brown in Houston, Texas, Neil Behan in Baltimore County, Maryland, and Darrell Stephens in Newport News, Virginia, took the Commission's indictments seriously and inaugurated community policing and problem-oriented policing in their departments. Many regarded the development of community policing as the zenith of policing and a method that should be embraced wholesale by all departments. Unfortunately, in 1985 the crack decade began spawning unparalleled violence in American cities. As a result, by 1990 a new policing model began to evolve to bring order to the chaos.

Collective Police Wisdom

In many ways, the NYPD Crime Control Model (CompStat) is simple and obvious. This model incorporates modern management principles such that one wonders how the police could have missed it for so long. The Crime Control Model represents an integration of operations, functions, and resources for targeted reduction of crime.

The impetus for an integrated strategy of policing derived from experience and the serendipitous and simultaneous occurrences of the availability of technology, changing social conditions, and, most important, a new confidence in collective police wisdom. During the past 30 years, police have transformed themselves from a blue-collar category of workers to a profession. The police have gained higher education, some use of research and experimentation, management training, and experience managing highly complex systems. This experience and knowledge development allows the police to reform their structures, forms, and operations. Outside pressure for reform is no longer necessary, And it is important to note that the Crime Control Model evolved out of all that has gone before, including community policing.

The new, operational strategy involves changes in five functional areas: crime analysis, strategies and tactics, support units, command accountability, and community policing. High levels of development in one of these areas require work with the other four functional areas—one area can no longer function successfully without the other four. As one area changes, improves, and evolves, the other four change, improve, and evolve. Genuine interdependence is achieved. This process is outlined in Appendix A, Stages of Development of Police Operations.

Scientific Analysis of Crime Data

Parts of the NYPD Crime Control Model are beginning to appear in other police agencies as these agencies begin to rely on crime data for decisions. The Chicago Police Department is an example of an evolving strategy. The department has a strong and lasting commitment to community policing. The initial community policing strategy was based on a classic model of pushing decision-making responsibility to the police officers on the beat. Resources were devoted to training police officers to function as "the police chief of his or her beat" to create solutions to problems, work closely with neighborhood members, and, in conjunction with the public, select priorities for police and community attention. Eventually, crime analysis data and geo mapping technologies were made available to beat officers. Chicago officers were encouraged to share this information with the community so that, together, they could move from choosing priorities based on intuition, casual observations, and complaints to choosing priorities from quality analysis.

Once the process of scanning crime data was institutionalized, beat officers and sector sergeants observed that many problems were not confined to beats but often spanned patrol areas, sectors, districts, and even the city. Police personnel recognized that problems spanned or crossed area boundaries and required resources beyond the traditional capabilities of a patrol officer assigned to a beat. The Superintendent and the Deputy Chief developed a supplemental strategy that consisted of regular meetings between and among beat officers, sector sergeants, and district commanders. These meetings were expected to generate departmental strategies designed to solve identified problems that were beyond the resources and control of the single-beat officer. More recently, the Chicago Police Department transformed again to parallel the NYPD CompStat Model completely.

A similar change evolved in the Oakland, California, police department. The Oakland chief of police had organized the command staff by tours. One watch commander was responsible for the entire city from 8 A.M. to 4 P.M., a second from 4 P.M. to midnight, and a third from midnight until 8 A.M. As the department analyzed crime, commanders recognized that crime patterns did not occur by shifts or tours but, rather, throughout the day. The Oakland chief, in analyzing crime, quickly realized the problem and reorganized his patrol command by geographic area. Watch commanders were assigned to a geographic area and were held accountable for crime patterns and police responses throughout a 24-hour period. This change resulted in improved police response, more efficient use of resources, decline in identified crime patterns, and better communication among the command staff.

In the Columbus, Ohio, police department, another change is evolving. In implementing community policing, the Columbus chief of police established a new entity entitled the Strategic Response Bureau. Within the bureau, community liaison officers were assigned to each of 18 precincts. The crime analysis unit was placed in the Strategic Response Bureau, as was one group of officers assigned to enforcement and another group assigned to investigations. The Bureau targets crime patterns that are not confined to beats and that require resources beyond patrol. The Bureau combines analysis, assessment, and tactical response based on defined strategies. The crime analysis unit now distributes crime pattern information throughout the department. Based on this information, patrol may request the Bureau's assistance.

CHANGES IN THE NYPD CRIME CONTROL MODEL

The NYPD has gained national recognition for breaking with traditional approaches and implementing a crime control model that has resulted in reduced crime and renewed vigor toward community development. Building on the NYPD's community policing strategy, the police commissioner instituted changes characterized by a relentless commitment to improving neighborhoods and communities. Other police departments are replicating the NYPD Crime Control Model. The CompStat Model is characterized by frequent scientific analysis of crime data, command accountability, creative strategies and tactics in response to identified crime patterns and by availability and immediate application of support services and resources. Clifford Krauss, in a recent *New York Times* article, described the model applied to a drug initiative in Brooklyn:

> *The old divisions between patrol officers, detectives, and narcotics investigators are disappearing enabling a single precinct to take a team approach. And the department is working more closely with Federal agencies than ever before . . . The drug trade in Northern Brooklyn is mostly retail and on a small scale, but Mr. Bratton decided to test a pet theory, that the police department's structure of separate narcotics, detectives, patrol and housing police commands was woefully inefficient in reducing crime that was for the most part driven by the drug trade.*[1]

The NYPD used crime data to analyze hot spots, then eliminated traditional organizational barriers to allow the precinct commander to bring together all resources needed to affect change. The approach has proven highly effective in various areas and in response to a wide array of problems.

CHANGES FOR THE PATROL COMMANDER ROLE

An important change that emerged from the crime control model was improved accountability of higher-ranking patrol commanders. In the past, most commanders in patrol viewed their jobs as primarily administrative. Their administrative roles were reinforced by community policing as the beat officer became the central element of problem solving and crime resolution in the police department while community policing encouraged partnership with the community, but it also reinforced an isolation from the patrol commander. One study in a large police department described the current jobs of managers and supervisors and outlined needed changes:

> [They] have a responsibility to convey information, to provide guidance and leadership to their subordinates. Daily this means they have to make decisions about scheduling, operational activities, performance evaluation, etc. Sometimes this includes having to take negative disciplinary action . . . Sergeants should receive training so they can: - be more involved with what is going on in the street. They (sergeants) should have precise information on officer workload; - participate in problem solving and coach officers through the process if needed; - help officers find ways to improve problem analysis; - provide officers with ways to upgrade their problem solving and community engagement skills; - make sure that problem solving efforts are evaluated for effectiveness; - make sure problem solving efforts are documented so others can learn from the effort; - and evaluate personnel on the basis of problem solving and community involvement success.

In this department, sergeants have an active role in managing police officers, whereas lieutenants, captains, and patrol commanders are just beginning to become more involved. In the past, traditional job descriptions of patrol commanders rarely, if ever, covered responsibility for crime control and reduction, for designing and carrying out strategies and tactics, for analyzing and using crime and other data to identify and solve problems, and for facilitating the use of support services and resources to support the problem-solving efforts of officers. In the NYPD, Columbus police, Oakland police, and others, change is taking place in how the role of manager/leader is defined. One of the first departments to require that its patrol commanders assume responsibility for crime control was the NY Transit Police Department. Clear objectives were established for commanders with the primary focus on reducing crime and maintaining order. Specialty units were directed to support patrol as their first and only priority. The Transit Police crime analysis unit provided crime pattern and hot spot identification on a daily basis through special alerts. The crime analysis unit also chaired a meeting every other week between commanders in the patrol and detective bureaus to ensure coordinated efforts.

The two bureaus, patrol and criminal investigations, were held accountable for developing strategies and tactics in response to the crime patterns. This forced another significant change. The role of the detective was enhanced because those individuals assigned to investigations were challenged, for the first time, to create strategies and play a part in their implementation. In the New York, Indianapolis, and Baltimore police departments, commanders are responsible and accountable for crime control in their areas, and the retention of their positions depends on success. In these departments, commanders identify, implement, and evaluate their work. Lack of interest, inadequate performance, or failure to cooperate with other units can result in transfer or demotion. This represents one of the first times that police commanders have been held accountable for productivity and outcomes in a manner similar to that of their executive counterparts in the private or corporate sector.

LONG-TERM IMPACT ON LAW ENFORCEMENT

Although thorough external evaluation of the NYPD CompStat program has not yet been conducted, some regard this program as "tipping point" in the dramatic decrease in crime in New York City. When the program was introduced in the NYPD, considerable community organization directed at restoring order had already occurred. The Midtown Manhattan Drug Court was operating along with other experimental court programs to prosecute misdemeanor crimes. The dramatic decrease in crime did not occur, however, until the police activities and resources were reorganized under CompStat. CompStat has this effect on crime because it integrates all police functions, increases productivity, and improves the overall effectiveness of the police. More than one third of major cities in the United States have begun to adopt and adapt the CompStat program in their police departments.

This method of efficient and well-managed police service has long-term implications for the profession:

- *In the future, police managers will require more sophisticated and complex training and preparation.* Today's mid-level managers aspiring to top-level leadership roles should prepare themselves with complex and sophisticated skills such as (a) the ability to analyze data scientifically; (b) the ability to create, develop, and apply a variety of tactics and strategies; (c) an understanding of theories of command; (d) the ability to coordinate resources of several functional units and other government agencies in concert with elements of the community; (d) skills in tracking, monitoring, adjusting, and evaluating singular and multidimensional crime control activities; and (e) the ability to track and draw important conclusions from trend analysis.

- *Entry-level police curriculum will need similar revision so recruits will fit into the new operations and procedures.*

- *Community policing will experience a new level of acceptance and importance.* The CompStat program has the potential to integrate community policing into the entire crime control program. Thus, officers will be held accountable in more effective ways, and departmental resources will be available to facilitate the jobs of officers within the community context.

- *There will be a clear and unmistakable demarcation between those departments managed at higher levels of complexity and efficiency and those departments operating in more traditional ways.* These new, professional police departments operating on the basis of scientific analysis of data, with the integration of functions and resources, and held accountable for successful outcomes will deliver strong and vigorous police services. Other communities will begin to demand a like level of effectiveness.

SUMMARY

The new crime control program evolved and developed from a need to solve complex and urgent problems, coupled with new experiences, experimentation, partnering and a freedom of thought. The police profession has a right to be proud—for this was all accomplished through their own collective police wisdom.

Note

1. "Brooklyn Drug Sweeps Begin to Make Inroads," *New York Times,* May 10, 1996.

CHAPTER EIGHT

The New Approach to Performance Management

I n many respects this entire book has been about the changes in the interrelationships among performance management, accountability, and police operations management. In the 1990s, major conceptual shifts in performance evaluation directly affected accountability and operations.

In the past, whenever "performance evaluation" was mentioned, everyone automatically thought of evaluation of individual workers. Now, a revolution in both policing and government has changed this perception. This is referred to as a "revolution" rather than as evolution because major conceptual shifts occurred rapidly over an eight-year period, which resulted in profound alterations in how both government and police conduct business. These major shifts occurred in government and policing nearly simultaneously but also nearly independent of each other. This chapter will explain the nature of the shifts and trace their history in policing and government.

THE POLICE PERFORMANCE MANAGEMENT EARTHQUAKE— THE NATURE OF THE CONCEPTUAL SHIFTS

Eight major conceptual changes occurred in policing and government in the 1990s. These shifts occurred in seemingly separate and unrelated functions and, ultimately, led to an overall change in focus from individual performance evaluation to agency performance management.

From Outputs to Outcomes

The most significant functional change was the movement from measuring "outputs" to measuring "outcomes." For years, both police and government standards were rated on outputs, and now one wonders why it took so long to realize that results are far more important than is work productivity, that is, outputs. Today, modern government agencies and police measure their success on the basis of results achieved, not by productivity levels.

In policing, success is gauged by levels of public safety and fear of crime. In the past, individual police officers were rated by the number of arrests (quota), the number of traffic tickets issued, or the pounds of illegal substances seized. Today, the competent chief and his or her personnel are rated on whether or not serious crime issues are under control and whether or not the fear level is high or low. In turn, the modern police executive delves into and oversees the work of commanders to ensure that results are achieved at the problem-solving level. The problems identified through data must be solved; the police executive is no longer content with the number of arrests. For example, suppose an effort is made to remove abandoned buildings, and the drug dealers who use them, from the community. The modern police executive would be less interested in the number of buildings leveled or the number of drug dealers incarcerated than in whether the effort has increased neighborhood safety.

Another example of this principle is a research project funded by the National Institute of Justice, U.S. Department of Justice, and being conducted by Abt Associates. The goal is to develop outcome measures for multijurisdictional task forces (MJTF). State planning agencies funding MJTFs began to understand that the number of pounds of cocaine seized did not reveal whether an area was more immune to drug trafficking or whether fewer teenagers were lured into drug habits. These state planning agencies wanted performance measures based on the outcomes of the MJTF. The research project is now focused on developing such measures.

Changing measures of success alters the driving force of the organization and its employees. Being more concerned about removing an open-air drug market from a neighborhood than about arresting individuals to meet a quota affects the strategic planning of involved officers. One need only think of the kinds of questions that each of these measures of success provokes. For example, when a police officer has been given an arrest quota, he or she might ask these questions: How can I find potential arrestees? Where might they be located and what might they be doing? Can I meet my quota this month? Once I meet my quota, can I relax? Compare these questions with the types of questions that an outcome-driven employee has: What data is available to correctly identify problems and issues in my neighborhood area? What data is available that can be analyzed to develop tactics and strategies? What are the most appropriate strategies and what other offices or agencies do I need to work with to successfully apply the strategies? What data is available to indicate if the problem has been solved or if the strategy needs revision to solve the problem?

Further, tactics that will permanently remove an open-air drug market involve more agencies than the local police department, such as Public Works, Legal Counsel, or Landlord and Tenant Office, whereas planning to increase number of arrests involves only the police department, that is, plain clothes officers, decoys, and stings. The first strategy has more potential to permanently clean up a neighborhood, whereas the second tends to motivate drug sellers to be creative about avoiding the police.

Other impacts of using outcomes rather than outputs as measures of success are the following:

- Outcome-driven management tends to unite previously disparate and separate police units for more effective and comprehensive approaches. For example, if a drug unit and a patrol unit act independently within a geographic area, their activities could be counterproductive, and their overall impact could be diminished. By working together, however, the two units coordinate their activities to become more effective.

- Outcome-driven management provides a different and positive level of satisfaction. Satisfaction in seeing that a neighborhood is safer, cleaner, and able to reclaim its streets is an intrinsic satisfaction, whereas the satisfaction accrued from meeting an arrest quota is highly temporary because the officer must achieve the same quota all over again next week or month. Humans derive comfort from intrinsic satisfaction. This type of satisfaction as the result of creative planning produces a police department whose motivation is improving public safety. Meeting arrest quotas produces an agency subject to corruption and rules violations to serve the "master."

Remember, in policing, the shift from outputs to outcomes as measures of success could be deemed an accident of nature. In Chapter 1, we saw how the NY Transit Authority was desperate and the new chief was told that he had one year to reduce robberies, fare evasions, and disorder on the subway. Interestingly, as other chiefs saw how more efficient and effective management could reduce crime, many followed the NY example. When an agency moves to outcome-driven management, the changes described also occur in rapid succession.

From Incidents to Problems

The need to successfully solve problems leads to the recognition that continuously responding to the same address wastes valuable police resources. When, however, the officer or team analyzes the problem related to the address and takes steps to solve the problem, resources are conserved and public safety and outcomes are more readily achieved. This conceptual shift actually began in 1978 when some researchers analyzed Boston Police Department calls for service and discovered that 70 percent of the calls derived from the same 10 percent of addresses. However, the knowledge was not effectively converted to police operations until the 1990s.

As a result of the CompStat process another shift occurred. Police executives began to solve problems at individual locations, to group locations in close proximity, and to identify the causative factors related to a geographic area. With this approach, comprehensive solutions are designed to eliminate the underlying causes.

From Summary Results to Feedback

Simultaneously, as strategic decisions were developed on the basis of data rather than intuition or some other decision-making criteria, the importance of regular and interim feedback was recognized. Police executives began to understand that it was wasteful to identify a problem, amass police resources to solve the problem, and then not check the results. Early monitoring of results could lead to changes in the strategy if positive results were not forthcoming. Monitoring can also lead to terminating the strategy when desired results are achieved. Too often in the past, both police and government have established "programs" to attack a specific problem. The programs then tended to go on indefinitely, as routines were established, personnel became wedded to new positions, and results were not checked. One impact of continuous and ongoing feedback is a new urgency that produces dramatic results. This maturation of the analysis process also conserves resources.

From Reaction to Prevention

There is a vast difference between traditional policing, such as responding to calls and chasing down and arresting the perpetrator, to new understandings of prevention. In the past, crime prevention consisted of teaching individuals how to protect themselves from potential offenders. For today's police, prevention is a comprehensive strategy to ensure safety in a neighborhood. Modern police identify the problem or problem area and design a strategy to stop the immediate threat and potential harm and ensure that the area is not vulnerable to future criminal activities.

From Control of Serious Crime to Public Safety

As all the other conceptual shifts occurred and a gradual maturation of the police evolved, items measured shifted as well. In the past, the focus was often categories of serious crimes; today there is a concern for overall safety. Police are interested in knowing the citizens' perceptions of fear and safety and the prevalence of disorder. Public safety comprises all these measures. This is not to say that measures of serious crime are not important. For those cities and areas where a type of serious crime, generally well-publicized, harms a city's well-being, particularly economic, it makes sense to be concerned with serious crime statistics. Similarly, when a city begins to increase safety in neighborhoods, serious crime statistics become the bellringer of that increased safety. Ultimately, cities should use all three measures—serious crime, disorder, and fear—to take the temperature of public safety.

From Accountability for Rules to Accountability for Problems Solved

For many years, the only system of accountability in police agencies was the Internal Affairs Department or internal investigations of the violation of rules, policies, and procedures since rules violators are responsible for corruption and the public's decreased trust in police services. Today a new type of accountability system is in place. These accountability systems cannot be ignored and must still function. Additional accountability systems are now in place—accountability systems that hold members responsible for solving problems and contributing to public safety.

From Individual Attribute-Based Performance Evaluation to Unit or Agency Performance Management

This conceptual shift is key to new approaches to operations and improved results. In the past, both government and police expended tremendous amounts of energy to develop effective individual performance evaluations. Some government functions, such as the U.S. Army, eventually abandoned the quest. Finally, police departments recognized that rating individuals on attributes was fine but did not contribute to improved performance. Departments created elaborate and more time-consuming systems to track, monitor, and rate actual work of individuals. Although conceptually this newer system moved departments closer to understanding the issues of an individual related to actual performance, the time required to manage such a system was inordinate. Many of these systems ultimately resorted to short cuts and reduced actual observations of work. Thus, the results are similar to the individual evaluations based on attributes—not very helpful. Many of the older evaluation systems have given way to new accountability that hold members and units responsible for increasing public safety.

From Intuition to Data

The role of technology changed as a result of the shift from outputs to outcomes. New technologies allow the accumulation of massive amounts of data for overall and comprehensive analysis of results and real-time data availability. These new technologies contribute to the substantial change in police management and should be considered essential to the new performance management approaches. Viewing a graphic that represents numerous data points summarized and classified facilitates a broader view of the problems plaguing a neighborhood than hands-on patrol waiting to encounter problems. In addition, real-time data allows managers to chart progress in small increments, which then contributes to alterations in strategies and tactics more rapidly.

Too many theorists discuss performance measurement and management as though it were an isolated function. The new systems, however, ensure that performance is tightly related to strategies developed to solve identified problems in three ways: by demanding continuous and ongoing feedback on results, by shifting emphasis based on available data, and by tying results to individuals, units, or agency. Performance management and measurement is no longer isolated from work activities but, rather, is an integral part and critical to overall public safety. Graphically, these ideas may appear as shown in Table 8-1. Police executives no longer think or speak of performance evaluation on the one hand and police activities and accountability on the other—evaluation, activities, and accountability are inextricably linked.

Mark Moore provides a further integration in his recent paper: *Recognizing and Realizing Public Value in Policing: The Challenge of Measuring Police Performance.*[1] Moore discusses "external" and "internal" accountability systems. He dscribes the police as being accountable to their authorizing environment, which he depicts as "all those actors who have the formal power to comment on and review police department operations, or who have the informal power to influence those who do." Moore goes on to say that the police should be accountable to that external environment insofar as the problems to be solved are negotiated between the police and the external environment. Ultimately, measures are derived from police activities relating to the negotiated issues. This implies that those measures reported to the external environment for external accountability are related to internal accountability, which Moore also describes as the only means by which a "police chief can actually have any chance of driving the organization to high levels of performance." And, continues Moore, "the first, and most important, is the extent to which the internal system of performance measurement is aligned with the external reporting system."

From Isolation to Integration

To understand the shift from performance evaluation to performance management, one must recognize and understand how police executives now view their departments, responsibilities, and operations. A fragmented view of operations and performance measurement—wherein units operated in isolation, reported outputs as measures of success, and set their own individual objectives—has been replaced by a management system that includes cooperation between and among police units and city agencies, problems solved and safety ensured as measures of success, development of comprehensive strategies, continuous and ongoing oversight of operations, and responsible commanders. This shift represents an extremely critical maturation wherein police executives view their departments and departmental activities with a broader and more holistic view. This new perspective on police operations provides new potential and power to influence crime and criminals and other components of the criminal justice system.

THE GOVERNMENT PERFORMANCE MANAGEMENT SHIFT

The federal government experienced a similar, though separate, awakening during the 1990s. The Clinton administration arrived in Washington, D.C., in 1993 with a reform agenda pertaining to the treatment of taxpayers. Clinton's agenda strongly

TABLE 8-1	**Public Safety**	
Status	**Police Activities**	**Measures**
Serious Crime	Apprehension and prevention strategies	Part I crimes
	Apprehension of offenders	Offenders incarcerated
Disorder	Cooperative programs with other agencies	Citizen calls/ complaints
	Public areas improved	Videos of areas
Fear	Improved public information	Citizen surveys
		Victimization surveys

reflected Tom Peters's writings of the late 1970s, in which Peters advocated that businesses carefully assess the needs of customers as a basis for shaping services. Clinton urged government services to begin with the "customer." "Most Federal workers were trapped in an industrial age assembly line where they passed paper from one office to the next."[2] The result was President Clinton's Executive Order 12862, "Setting Customer Service Standards."

Part of the movement toward serious and noticeable change was the notion of empowerment. "Empowerment works on two levels: the organizational and the individual."[3] Empowerment is functioning on the organizational level when all executives and workers agree on a mission and use the mission to drive decision making. Empowerment operates on the individual level when employees are given an opportunity to contribute creatively toward strategy development.

The new government also recognized that accountability had, in the past, only been concerned with identifying violators rather than focusing on problem solving.[4] Pursuit of violators as the primary means of accountability suggests two issues: (1) that a tremendous amount of energy is diverted from fulfilling the mission(s), and (2) that the violators are punished while the original problem is forgotten, leaving room for new violators to stumble over the same obstacles or issues.

Another ingredient of the government "sea" change is "getting results through learning."[5] One main concept that guides the creation of a learning environment is "Learning happens on the job everyday. Learning is adapting, and it is vital for the survival and well-being of the individual as well as the organization."[6]

Techniques advocated by the Human Resource Development Council[7] to foster a learning environment include the following:

- Meetings—Managers play the role of teacher by asking questions, demonstrating systems thinking, and discussing lessons learned.

- Action Learning—An actual problem in the work place is used for learning.

- Cross-Functional Teams—Individuals with different skills and backgrounds form a team to bring a wide range of viewpoints to some task.

- Workouts—Teams composed of a broad spectrum of employees at all levels meet without management to seek answers to business problems.

- Strategic Planning—Strategies include measures of success to determine whether or not the problem has been solved.
- Corporate Scorecards—These provide a means to track measurements that are important to the success of the organization. (pages 19–21)

Another business theorist, Jim Collins, ties the learning organization to accountability through the use of a concept he terms "catalytic mechanism." According to Collins, catalytic mechanisms are devices that transform lofty aspirations into concrete reality.[8] Essentially this technique, similar to federal government actions, allows line employees to participate in creating sound solutions to identified problems. The focus in the catalytic mechanism becomes one of identifying means to link employees to results, removing any doubts about their purpose and the goals they should be pursuing.

Theorists in government, industry, and policing alike have arrived at the conclusion that both employees and operations must be marshaled to achieve results or outcomes. This notion was operationalized by the U.S. Congress with the passage of the Government Performance and Results Act (GPRA) of 1993."[9] Examples of federal government agencies that identified outcomes as goals successfully are illustrated in Table 8-2.

This federal government transformation is not occurring without difficulties. J. Christopher Mihm, of the U.S. General Accounting Office (GAO) has identified two major stumbling blocks that apply also to police agencies converting to CompStat:

1. "Understanding how an agency's programs and strategies contribute to results. Results are effects that occur outside an organization. Thus, on a daily basis, agencies do not create results but, rather, provide products and services that in turn contribute to results. However, very few agency performance plans demonstrated the vital understandings of how strategies, processes, and programs contribute to the achievement of results . . . Simply stated, an agency cannot improve performance if it does not have a clear understanding of how what it does now contributes to current levels of performance (the achievement of outcomes)."

2. "Ensuring that performance data will be credible for decision making. The Results Act requires agencies in their performance plans to discuss how performance data will be verified and validated. However, the GAO found that few agencies did an acceptable job in this regard. In fact, the inattention to ensuring that performance data will be sufficiently timely, complete, and accurate is one of the greatest weaknesses that GAO has consistently seen across all agencies' plans. This suggests that performance reporting in many agencies will be compromised by a lack of quality data."[10]

Whether it was a coincidence or not, the book *Reinventing Government,*[11] which provided the theory behind the GPRA movement, was published in 1993. David Osborne and Ted Gaebler describe the advantages of mission-driven organizations as being: "(1) more efficient than rule-driven organizations; (2) more effective . . . they produce better results; (3) more innovative than rule-driven organizations; (4) more flexible; and (5) having higher morale."[12] Osborne and Gaebler describe why organizations are more effective when they are driven by missions instead of by

TABLE 8-2	Federal Government Agencies That Have Identified Oucomes as Goals		
Agency	**Strategic Goal**	**Intermediate Goal**	**End Outcomes**
National Highway Safety and Traffic Administration (NHTSA)	Promote the public health and safety by working to eliminate transportation-related deaths, injuries, and property damage	Increase rate of front seat safety belt use. Reduce number of alcohol-related fatalities	Reduce rates of transportation-related fatalities and injuries per 100 million vehicle miles traveled
Title 1: Education Assistance Program	At-risk students improve achievement to meet challenging academic content and performance standards	States adopt challenging performance standards. Schools improve teacher training and curriculum and instruction and extend learning time	Increase mathematics and reading test scores among children in high-poverty schools

unit autonomy through a vignette describing government services in New York City; "If a rat is found in an apartment, it is a housing inspection responsibility; if it runs into a restaurant, the health department has jurisdiction; if it goes outside and dies in an alley, the public works department takes over."[13] In other words, if the three separate organizations had as an objective to rid the city of rats and collaborated to achieve this objective, this ineffective division of labor would not occur.

Osborne and Gaebler elaborate on the inefficiency that transpires when agencies use data for decision making and do not measure results. Stakeholders cannot tell success from failure—decisions tend to get made on the basis of who has the most political influence; when programs are cut, one cannot tell which is being sliced off, fat or lean. The authors even discuss the police: "Police forces make this mistake all the time. Research proves that doubling the number of patrol cars on the street has no effect on the levels of crime—or on public anxiety about crime. Yet, when crime rates rise, the police buy more squad cars."[14] And finally, Osborne and Gaebler succinctly point out that if you cannot recognize failure, you cannot correct it.[15]

Management of Cities

The move to data and accountability-driven management is occurring in cities as well as in police agencies and the federal government, but at a slower pace. Several cities are exploring the use of outcomes/goals to manage city operations.[16] These cities are taking steps to identify outcomes as achievement objectives but are not following through by establishing an interactive process—involving department or unit heads—to ensure that outcomes are pursued in an effective manner.

TABLE 8-3	Changes in Movements in Policing and Government in the 1990s

Government	Police
Customer focus	Focus on solving crime problems in neighborhoods
Empowerment	Involving officers at all levels to design strategies, e.g., precinct problem-solving teams
Concerns with achieving results	Direct review of strategy impact on problems in neighborhoods
Learning, the central focus	CompStat meetings and precinct problem-solving meetings become learning experiences for all attendees and participants
Catalytic mechanisms to connect goals	Series of meetings at command level and other rank levels to develop strategies and tactics, which are reviewed for objective achievement or problem solutions
Performance management— a focus on outcomes rather than outputs	Success is measured by whether or not a precinct solves a neighborhood problem rather than by number of arrests or traffic tickets issued

These cities continue to use traditional reporting practices and require report-back annually. (Indianapolis is an exception and requires agencies to report results monthly.[17])

Some city and government officials have difficulty understanding and applying outcome measures. Often, administrative goals and agency outcomes are confused. For example, the Nova Scotia Department of Human Resources defines outcome measures as performance management for employees, decreased absenteeism, healthy work environment, and a diverse workforce.[18] These are not "outcomes" in work accomplished by the agency but, rather, desired changes in the function of internal administration. These objectives, as stated, represent outcomes to be achieved by administrative management only. Most workers and operational supervisors/managers can do little to implement these programs. In contrast, outcome goals must be related to the core work of the agency and, thus, provide direction for all workers. For example, the Australian Queensland Community Housing Coalition has established community integration, poverty alleviation, and tenant empowerment as its outcome goals.[19]

Although these outcome goals are too broad in many respects for effective targeting, they identify critical issues that all agency employees can work to solve.

Government and Police

Table 8-3 compares the changes in movements during the 1990s in both policing and government.

SUMMARY

Both government and the police have taken enormous strides to improve how they conduct their separate and distinct businesses and to provide greater satisfaction for the American citizen. This book has already described the types of skills and abilities that the police manager of the future will have to possess to manage an effective police organization, but what of the overall nature of policing? If technology and new approaches to management allow a police department to function at a higher and more effective level of achievement, then we would assume that different levels of service would be available and that a shift from setting goals around crime reduction to creating public safety would occur. When the shift to public safety occurs, then the police must search for new partners. School systems, public health agencies, social service agencies, and any other unit within a jurisdiction that has related con-

cerns, focusing on the same objective or mission, will cooperate with the police and the criminal justice system.

This concept is becoming operationalized in Seattle, Washington. A program, COMPASS (funded by the U.S. National Institute of Justice), begins with the accumulation of data from all relevant agencies. This data will be analyzed for problems that are common to more than one agency. Cooperative strategies will then be developed to solve the problems. What COMPASS needs to function like a CompStat agency is for the program to establish a board responsible for reviewing actions and strategies in regularly scheduled, open meetings that hold agencies accountable. (This feature of COMPASS is not yet part of the planning process.) The final outcome will be a learning jurisdiction with great potential to establish and maintain public safety.

Notes

1. Moore, Mark. *Recognizing and Realizing Public Value in Policing: The Challenge of Measuring Police Performance,* Fall, 2001. Washington, DC: PERF

2. Vice-President Al Gore. *Business-Like Government: Lessons Learned from America's Best Companies*, 1997 (October). Washington, DC: National Performance Review, U.S. Government Printing Office, page 7.

3. Ibid, page 10.

4. Ibid, page 35.

5. Ibid, page XX

6. Ibid, page 79.

7. Human Resource Development Council. *Getting Results Through Learning,* 1997 (June). Washington, DC: U.S. Government Printing Office.

8. Collins, Jim. "Turning Goals Into Results: The Power of Catalytic Mechanisms," *Harvard Business Review,* July–August, 1999, pages 71–82.

9. *Government Accounting Office Managing for Results: Measuring Program Results That Are Under Limited Federal Control,* 1998. Washington, DC: U.S. Government Printing Office.

10. Mihm, J. Christopher. "Getting Ready for Performance Reporting," *Public Manager,* 1999. Potomac, MD, page 7.

11. Osborne, David, and Ted Gaebler. *Reinventing Government: How the Entrepreneurial Spirit Is Transforming the Public Sector,* 1993. New York: Plume.

12. Ibid, pages 111–112.

13. Ibid, page 132.

14. Ibid, pages 147–148.

15. Ibid, page 152.

16. Cities include Seattle, Washington; Indianapolis, Indiana; Phoenix, Arizona; Austin, Texas.

17. Moynihan, Donald P. *Managing for Results in Cities: Innovative Practices;* Maxwell School of Citizenship and Public Affairs—Syracuse

University, Syracuse, New York; March 2000: http://www.maxwell.syr.edu/gpp/mrfresearch .htm

18. Nova Scotia Department of Human Resources, 2000. *Highlights of Outcome Measures;* www.gov.ns.ca/humr/nscounts/outcome/htm.

19. Community Housing Forum. "Social Outcomes—New Forms of Performance Management," *Newsletter of the National Community Housing Forum,* Vol.3, Issue 3, Sept. 1998.

Stages of Development of Police Functional Areas[1]

This appendix outlines the developmental stages of seven functional units as a department progresses from a traditional policing model through community policing to a modern, data-driven, results-oriented model.

[1] McDonald, Phyllis. Unpublished document, National Institute of Justice, U.S. Department of Justice, 1997.

Stages of Development of Police Functional Areas

Crime Analysis

Stage 1

Department or crime analysis unit collects crime data; prepares data summaries over varying but regular time periods (e.g., quarterly, semiannually, or annually); distributes reports to select number of policy/decision makers (e.g., mayor, chief, budget or patrol commanders).

Stage 2

Department or crime analysis unit collects crime data; makes more frequent reports; distributes reports to broader audience (e.g., all commanders, some community groups). Gross and comprehensive crime trends (e.g., those for serious crimes) may be tracked and compared with previous years; focus may be on specific crimes (e.g., homicides).

Stage 3

Occurs in conjunction with a community-oriented policing program. Crime data is analyzed regularly (e.g., monthly, weekly, daily), most often by beat area to identify hot spots, which might be identified only by individual beat officers for their areas. There is no central crime analysis unit, but data might be communicated to neighborhood residents.

Stage 4

Includes comprehensive data collection/reporting and identification of hot spots in beat areas. Centralized crime unit identifies hot spots and crime patterns frequently and regularly (e.g., weekly, daily) and communicates results rapidly to patrol commanders, other commanders, and chief so they can develop strategies and tactics and chart progress in clearing crime patterns and hot spots. Data is used to hold commanders and others accountable; electronic pin mapping is used.

Strategy and Tactics Development

Stage 1

Broad-scale, typical patrol strategies are used, but members perform them in isolation from each other (e.g. random patrol, arrests, check locks for businesses, answer calls for service). Special police action might be invoked for areas that produce numerous calls for service (e.g., public hous-

Stage 2

Problem solving occurs by beat area, around problems generally identified by individual officers or community members, or problem solving might be driven solely by complaints of citizens. Officers most often operate alone or with neighborhood members, are not held accountable for activities or

Stage 3

Precinct or district commander is responsible for either prioritized crime types or all crime in his or her district, begins to identify "hot spots" in his or her area, begins to form teams to develop strategies and tactics, and begins to request support unit assistance in implementing a strategy.

Stage 4

Commanders are held accountable for crime in their districts and must report progress regularly to a patrol commander or chief of police. Crime patterns and hot spots are reported to all district commanders frequently by a centralized crime analysis unit. Support units assist commanding, teen hangouts, intensive drug-dealing areas). No member of the department is held responsible; success or failure is immaterial.

progress, but are responsible for selecting problems and implementing solutions. Shifting priorities cause uneven performance and success rates; departments can progress and become more organized and selective if crime data is supplied regularly.

Commander may begin to evaluate impact using crime data.

ers in planning creative and varied strategies to attack crime patterns. Commanders regularly evaluate interventions, either independently or with a departmental team, to judge impact of interventions.

Organizational Location and Applications of Support Units

Stage 1

Support units operate in isolation from each other and from the patrol force and respond to calls relevant to the type of support unit (e.g., canine units pursue a robber or track a lost child, SWAT teams manage a hostage scene, narcotics units investigate a drug dealer). Units usually report to criminal investigations, technical support, or special services bureau, but records of activities and success of interventions are rarely kept. Units usually react to events as they occur, occasionally set output objectives.

Stage 2

Officials begin to assess the jurisdiction for developing problems to determine which unit might be able to intervene (e.g., a drug unit discovers a burgeoning drug market and begins stake outs and other means to interrupt sales). Support units will report numbers of successes (e.g., number of arrests or amount of drugs taken off street), set their own objectives, and begin to track trends.

Stage 3

Support units develop loose arrangements with patrol units to respond when there is down time from pursuing the support units' own objectives.

Stage 4

Support unit objectives are derived from the overall mission or priorities of department. Support units are responsible to patrol commander, fill requests of district commanders for resources, may be part of a problem-solving team to design strategies for an identified crime pattern or hot spot. Commanders regularly analyze interventions for successes and failures so they can develop improvements.

Role of District Commander

Stage 1

The district commander is responsible for administration

Stage 2

The district commander begins to have some input into per-

Stage 3

District commander may begin to attend community meet-

Stage 4

District commanders are responsible for the design,

Continued

of the district or precinct but is not involved in decisions regarding personnel changes, transfers, and so forth—only the paper work pertaining to such changes. The commander communicates new policies and procedures to subordinates and may be responsible for communicating and enforcing decisions of the Internal Affairs Department. The commander's performance is only evaluated perfunctorily. The district commander is not consulted about changes in policies and procedures of any other major departmental decisions.

sonnel decisions, may be given some responsibility for budget expenditures, may be involved in departmental planning and development of policies and procedures, and may be involved in conducting investigations of citizen complaints and rendering decisions about punishment of guilty officers.

creation, and implementation of crime strategies for a geographical area over a 24-hour period, organizing teams of officers as appropriate for strategy development. District commanders are responsible for working with other commanders and jurisdictional members when crime patterns stretch beyond their districts, for resource allocation and deployment on a daily basis depending on crime data, for detection and arrest for all types of crimes, for receiving and using crime data from a centralized unit frequently, for developing strategies in response to patterns and hot spots, for supervising the conduct of community-oriented policing in appropriate areas and times, and for deploying support units in service of strategies.

Community Policing Strategy

Stage 1

A separate unit is established to respond to community concerns. Officers can do "community-oriented policings, establishes community policing officers, ensures that crime data is available to individual officers, and ensures that officers receive data available to citizens in their beat areas.

Stage 2

One officer is assigned per beat area, working in isolation from the remainder of department but with neighborhood leaders

Stage 3

Beat officers receive crime data regularly to provide information to neighborhood groups and to serve as a basis

Stage 4

Officers in beat areas are involved in problem solving at several levels. Sector sergeants work as a team responsible

ing" only when they are not answering calls for service.

or members to address problems and concerns of the beat area. Officers might have access to crime data pertaining only to their beat areas. Problems may be selected based on loudest complainer.

for identifying "problems." Officers within a beat area assigned to individual shifts may be held accountable to work as a team to handle beat problems that span shift imes.

for crime patterns across sectors. District commanders work as teams responsible for crime patterns that span districts. Individual beat officers are responsible for working with citizens to solve problems indigenous to the beat area. The officer is also responsible for obtaining information from citizens that could pertain to crime patterns in the beat, sector, district, or city. Oversight is provided to coordinate community policing problems with available police resources; problem solutions are evaluated for results.

Criminal Investigations

Stage 1

Detectives respond to a patrol officer's report of a specific crime and begin the process of investigating the crime (e.g., take a second report, interviews the complainant, identifies potential witnesses and offenders, searches the crime scene for fingerprints and physical evidence). Detective units measures of success are largely productivity measures (e.g., arrests made, cases cleared).

Continued

Stage 2

The detective unit might be decentralized, or detectives might work in teams. Work might be micromanaged by the manager through weekly meetings to review progress; the manager begins to examine and analyze numbers of cases successfully prosecuted for improved report taking, evidence collection, and so forth.

Stage 3

Detectives work in teams and use computers to organize data or for case management. Detectives begin proactive operations by obtaining information through crime analysis about hot spots and patterns and use that information to develop actions to interrupt. In this stage, detectives begin to work with other specialized units. Success measures become more results oriented (e.g., numbers of cases successfully prosecuted) or analytical (e.g., numbers of witnesses interviewed or quality of evidence collected).

Stage 4

Criminal investigations commanders are in the same organization as the patrol commanders, and they typically work together to analyze hot spots and crime patterns. Detectives are assigned with patrol officers for proactive activities or prevention activities (e.g., decoy units, stake outs, undercover activities). Success measurements begin to revolve around numbers of incidences reduced or prevented, numbers of crime patterns rapidly interrupted, and numbers of hot spots resolved.

Disorder and Quality of Life

Stage 1

Neighborhood environmental symptoms are identified, curtailed, or eliminated, through the use of enforcement tactics (e.g., abandoned cars, loud noises, or weeds in vacant lots).

Stage 2

Causes of neighborhood environmental and behavioral disorder are identified, curtailed, or eliminated (e.g., teens congregating in a public space, street prostitution, street drug dealers, or housing used by drug dealers) through enforcement tactics.

Stage 3

Causes and symptoms of neighborhood environmental and behavioral disorders are identified, curtailed, or eliminated through police strategizing (e.g., events are targeted through the identification of crime patterns and through neighborhood feedback; appropriate strategies are then developed to solve problem). Government agencies and other law enforcement units are enlisted for broader, more comprehensive solutions to problems.

Stage 4

All stage three activities occur plus individuals engaging in disorderly behavior are detained, or arrested, and questioned to gather information to solve serious crimes.

Boston Police Department *CAM Newsletter* Excerpts

DECEMBER 1996, VOLUME 1.1

The following is a summary of different problem solving and prevention strategies discussed during the *bi-monthly Crime Analysis Meetings.* By sharing information with one another you may find some if not most of the problems you confront are also those experienced by your colleagues. Through cooperation the challenges that once seemed overwhelming now become manageable. These are just some of the innovative, practical, and useful strategies being practiced by a variety of police personnel on a daily basis.

District 14: Application of a Search Warrant for Graffiti Crimes

> *The intensive investigative effort applied to the graffiti problem . . . has yielded enough evidence to prosecute and secure punishment for those who commit this crime in our neighborhoods.*

Source: Boston Police Department, *CAM Newsletter,* Volume 1.1 (96-01), December 1996.

In November 1995, Sergeant Detective Kevin Mullen began an investigation of graffiti damage done to a newly erected stockade fence at the Stockyard Restaurant in Brighton. After photographing the extensive defacement, Sgt. Det. Mullen contacted Sergeant Nancy O'Laughlin of the MBTA's Police Department's Graffiti Squad who has several years of experience investigating these types of incidents. Sgt. O'Laughlin was able to identify the distinct "Exacto" tag on the Stockyard Restaurant as the work of a twenty-year-old Northeastern University student.

After further investigation, Sgt. Det. Mullen applied for and was granted a search warrant for Exacto's Allston apartment. This was the first graffiti related search warrant ever granted to a Boston Police Officer.

During the execution of the warrant, Sgt. Det. Mullen, Sgt. O'Laughlin and their teams seized more than seventy-five cans of spray paint, paint nozzles, face masks and sandpaper stickers, all tools of graffiti. They also seized a dozen scrapbooks, photo albums containing news clippings, sketches, and hundreds of photographs of graffiti damaged buildings. The detectives also seized videotapes capturing Exacto and his companions spray painting buildings. The photographs and videotapes were evidence that the individual had tagged property in New York City, Philadelphia, and Washington DC, as well as several locations in Boston.

After a very thorough search of Allston and Brighton, Sgt. Det. Mullen located Exacto's work on twenty-four separate buildings on this District and charged the individual with twenty-four counts of defacing property. On January 18, 1996, the defendant received an unprecedented sentence of six months house arrest (electronic bracelet), four years probation, 600 hours of community service; as well as one hundred dollars restitution to each of the twenty-four victims. This sentence, which was heard by a dozen local community activists and business owners who attended each court session sent a very loud message to other graffiti artists. It also told this community that we share their concerns about this problem, and will vigorously prosecute this kind of offender.

Since the successful apprehension and prosecution of Exacto, Sgt. Det. Mullen, Sgt. O'Laughlin and her partner, Detective Ivan Beremjo, have been able to identify three other major graffiti offenders on this district and have executed two additional search warrants. Those three individuals are currently awaiting trial. One of the three, who has been dubbed the "Hub's King of Graffiti" by the media is charged with seventy-seven counts of defacing property.

The intensive investigative effort applied to the graffiti problem in Allston-Brighton has identified four major adult offenders and has yielded enough evidence to prosecute and secure serious punishment for those who commit this crime in our neighborhoods.

District 2: Home Visits by Neighborhood Beat Officers in Domestic Violence Situations

By using a uniformed officer the message sent to the offender and victim is that police are serious about addressing the problem of domestic violence.

To address the number of repeat calls of domestic violence situations, the neighborhood beat officer (NBO) is used to provide their services as a form of a follow-up visit to the location. Once the initial call for a domestic violence situation is cleared by way of arrest, or by other means, the NBO then meets primarily with the victim and if available the suspect. Response by the NBO usually is one to two days after the incident. The main discussion revolves around the incident; also at this time the officer uses his or her desecration to refer the parties involved to proper counseling agencies. Once a follow-up has been made the NBO creates a form 26 to summarize the meeting. The form 26 is then sent to the supervising officer and kept on file. Currently approximately 90 percent of the designated beat area is specifically targeted in the business area, making it difficult to focus more of the NBO's efforts to the residential areas. Thus far home visits have proved to be an effective strategy, with the NBO's having to make only one additional follow-up visit. By using a uniformed officer the message sent to the offender and victim is that the police are serious about addressing the problem of domestic violence.

District 3: Form Storage Tool Kit

The "form storage tool kit" is an innovative method for organizing all commonly used Department forms which personnel who are assigned to neighborhood sectors store in their Department vehicle.

All necessary forms, checklists, citations, FIOs, sterile protective gloves, crime scene tape, etc., are supplied in a separate indexed hanging folder and compartments within a waterproof plastic storage bin. The tool kit is placed in the vehicle's trunk next to the spare tire. By organizing the forms in this fashion the officers are now able to retrieve this information within a minute's notice, without delay and confusion. Having the form tool kit readily available saves time and enables the officer to write the information in the field while the idea is still vivid in his or her memory.

Some of the more commonly used documents included in the form storage tool kit are:

Form 1.1 (Incident Report)

Form 1.1.1 (Continuation Sheet)

Form 6.1 (Activity Log)

Form 25 (Motor Vehicle Inspection Report)

Form 26 (Special Report)

209A: Domestic Abuse Law (Card)

Form 2012 (Motor Vehicle Inventory Form)

Registry of Motor Vehicles (White-E23 & Yellow-E65)

Violation/Citation/Notices

Hackney/Crime Prevention/FIOs

Form 2602b (Missing Person Report for NCIC Entry) requires signature of person reporting missing individual

District 6: Juvenile Diversion Program for Public Drinking Offenses

It is the goal of this program to make a real difference in the lives of those involved.

Public drinking by youths . . . the police answer to this complaint was "we are doing our job, we lock the kids up for public drinking and they pay a fine and are released." Normally, a juvenile is immediately released to a parent or guardian and maybe faces one or two court appearances along with a small fine. The opinion was that the police offered no real deterrent, which resulted in frustration for both police and community residents.

Sergeant Detective James Wyse, who was not a member of the Strategic Planning Team but sat in on several meetings, presented a document to the members that was the catalyst for change in addressing the problem. In addition to individual visits to all package stores to reinforce awareness of and compliance with the laws concerning sales to minors, delivery of kegs, and their documentation, proprietors were all put on notice that we would be conducting random sting operations to insure employees were not selling to minors. The major component of this document was the suggestion of a Juvenile Diversion Program for Public Drinking Offenses.

Planning team members Joseph Pagliarulo, ADA South Boston Court, Jack Leary, Probation Department South Boston Court, and Helen Allix, South Boston Against Drugs, took this recommendation and immediately laid the groundwork for implementation of the proposed program. Team members met several times with Sgt. Det. Wyse. As a result a Juvenile Diversion Program for First-Time Public Drinking was approved at the South Boston District Court. The basic program is as follows:

First time offenders, through their parent(s) or guardian(s), are given the option of taking the offense outside standard court procedures and instead participate in an alcohol awareness program. The offender as well as the parent(s) or guardian(s) must attend The South Boston Against Drugs program, which includes separate meetings during evening hours, that have a major impact on the social life of the youths. Dangers of alcohol use and abuse are discussed during the meetings. Every effort is made to deter the youths from alcohol. These sessions serve as a first time offender rehabilitation program. By including parents together with the youth a more informative experience is shared and this is considered the reason why the program became successful. There have been no repeat offenders among the initial 36 youths who were assigned to the program for the Summer of 1996.

Besides helping the police and improving the quality of life in the community it is hoped that the diversion program will have a positive impact on the life styles developed by the youngsters. "Hard drugs" get all the media attention, but in this community the number one drug problem is alcohol. It is the goal of this program to make a real difference in the lives of those involved.

Even without radical change the results of this program indicate that through creative problem solving we can make a tremendous difference. Partnerships as the one formed between Sgt. Det. Wyse, Joseph Pagliarulo, Jack Leary, and Helen Allix improve the effectiveness of the police. The Juvenile Diversion Program for Public Drinking Offenses has been made permanent through the South Boston Court. Its success has led to C6 officers meeting with Judge Concannon to address other areas of mutual concern.

FEBRUARY 1997, VOLUME 2.1

The following is a summary of different problem solving and prevention strategies discussed during the *bi-monthly Crime Analysis Meetings.* By sharing information with one another you may find some if not most of the problems you confront are also those experienced by your colleagues. Through cooperation the challenges that once seemed overwhelming now become manageable. These are just some of the innovative, practical, and useful strategies being practiced by a variety of police personnel on a daily basis.

District D-4: Operation BRAT (Burglary and Robbery Apprehension Team)

From the time the Operation began on September 31, 1996, the District experienced a decline in burglaries to 51 (44% decrease) with only 4 (61% decrease) occurring in the target area.

In the 30 days preceding September 04, 1996, Back Bay experienced an increase in burglaries with 13 incidents (90 occurring district wide), as did the South End with an increase in robberies also with 13 incidents (41 occurring district wide).

Through research of crime trends and statistics Captain Charles Cellucci and Lieutenant Detective William McCarthy placed the primary focus of efforts upon the time of day and the areas of highest occurrences. Through the meticulous examination of these crimes the Burglary and Robbery Apprehension Team was created. This team is composed of one superior officer and two plainclothes officers. Funding for this operation was achieved through use of overtime. Each day the supervisor of the team would be provided with a printout of crime associated with that area, an activity log, an unmarked vehicle as well as be briefed by Lt. Det. McCarthy. By conducting FIO's, arrests, and compiling 1-1 reports the team began an effective campaign in decreasing the amount of burglaries, and robberies.

From the time the Operation began on September 04, 1996, to when it ended on September 31, 1996, the District experienced a decline in burglaries to 51 (44 percent decrease) with only 4 (61 percent decrease) occurring in the target area. The number of robberies throughout the district remained the same at 41; however the target area reflected an 80 percent decline sustaining only 2 robberies. Success is made possible by the eagerness of the participating officers, who enjoyed the change of pace from doing details and being in uniform to being part of a plainclothes operation where the results could be measured. It must be kept in mind that

Source: Boston Police Department, *CAM Newsletter,* Volume 2.1 (97-01), February 1997.

this kind of operation is labor intensive, in that the units must remain in the target area and not be given any radio calls that would remove the officers from the operation.

District E-5: Operation Car Safe

After the initiation of Operation Car Safe the amount of car breaks decreased to 19, a difference of 76 to mark an 80% decrease, during the months of October 1, 1996, through January 16, 1997.

During October of 1996, the officers of District 5 continued in their efforts in controlling the incidents of car breaks. Operation Car Safe efforts were focused in business areas of West Roxbury, and Roslindale. Area sector cars and walking officers were assigned to the target areas on a daily basis. Officers focused their attention on vehicles that were unlocked; had personal property, a cellular phone in view; and or if the keys were left in the ignition. If one or more of these "violations" occurred the officer would place a Car Safe ticket on the vehicle. This would act as a reminder to the owner that the best way to handle a car break is to prevent a car break.

The information is stored in a database of reported car breaks. During October 01, 1995, through January 16, 1996, West Roxbury experienced 95 car breaks. After the initiation of Operation Car Safe the amount of car breaks decreased to 19, a difference of 76 to mark an 80 percent decrease, during the months of October 1, 1996, through January 16, 1997. A similar effect occurred in the target area of Roslindale. During October 01, 1995, through January 16, 1996, a total of 61 cars were broken into in Roslindale. From October 01, 1996, through January 16, 1997, Roslindale had a total of 43 car breaks, down 18 to mark a 30 percent decrease. In all, officers issued 272 Car Safe tickets during October 01, 1996 through January 16, 1997. Through the ardent use of Operation Car Safe, officers have built an awareness among the citizens which has led to positive results in crime reduction efforts.

District A-7: Operation Bonanza

From approaches such as these we create a lasting impression among those wanted individuals that the Department is relentless in pursuing.

In January of 1996, personnel from District 7 met with various law enforcement and city officials during an East Boston Safe Neighborhood Initiative meeting. During this meeting different approaches with respect to the annual warrant sweeps were discussed. Upon the suggestion of Assistant DA David Coffey to develop a sting operation, Sergeant Detective Donald Gosselin began the foundation that would lead to Operation Bonanza.

By contacting John Cloherty, Assistant Director of the MA Criminal History Board, a list of all East Boston residents who had outstanding warrants issued against them was forward to Sgt. Det. Gosselin. From this list the 1,100 names were placed into a mailing database which was created by using Microsoft Excel and Access. An official letterhead was created, which instructed the recipient to call a toll free phone number between April 08–13, 1996, to reserve their spot at the

"American Cable Survey Boston Location." This toll free number was set up in an improvised boiler room at District 7. To speak with those who did not speak English a bi-lingual officer was used to take incoming calls.

On April 02, 1996, the first mailing of 1,100 letters was executed. To accomplish this Cadet Marino, Cadet Schepeci, and Detective Clerk Marilyn Golisano assisted in physical aspects of the mailing. With regard to a return address, a post office box was used for mailing responses. Despite the explicit instructions to call during the designated dates, recipients of the letters began to call on April 03, 1996. Captain Cunningham decided to immediately place Officer Palomares on duty to field calls. As a precaution, all personnel were told that radios were restricted from use on the second floor of the station. Turing off the intercom on the second floor also added to the security of the operation. By the week ending April 13, 32 people had reserved their place in the survey. Voice mail was used towards the end of the week to inform people that all survey slots had been filled, in order for them to be notified in case of cancellations they were told to leave their name and phone numbers. From the list of 32 a second mailing was created consisting of a survey admission ticket, a MBTA parking pass, and a letter with directions and explanation. To further the accommodation of mass arrest and ensure safety the arrival times were placed into 3 time categories.

Sergeant Detective Joe Finandaca was asked to plan, staff, and execute the takedown phase of this operation. Joseph Lawless, Director of Public Safety at Massport was contacted and offered a location to conduct the operation. A free shuttle was offered to the participants; this enable the officers heightened control over the targets and minimized resistance. Detectives Wyzard and Gavin were chosen as a driver and greeter. Observation of the targets was streamlined by seating an officer (acting as a survey taker) towards the rear of the shuttle. An unmarked white van was provided by Fleet Management, all police markings and blue lights were removed, however when the van was picked up the police radio was still intact. The radio was hidden by placing a jacket over it.

A pre-operation briefing was given at District 7 that included only those immediately involved in the operation. Officer Donald Stone initiated a discussion regarding a history of those targeted. Comments about each respective target and the likelihood of the use of violence, weapons possession, and resistance was outlined. The Survey Team arrived at the site approximately 20 minutes early to set up and 3 of the targets were already there waiting. At the site the easels and balloons were displayed to enhance the appearance of professionalism. Additionally, those in the Survey Team were dressed in the appropriate business attire. One drawback noted in the operation was that the issued BPD cellular telephones did not receive incoming calls. To overcome this obstacle Sgt. Det. Gosselin contacted District 7 and advised the desk to contact the Takedown Team by radio to inform them of the Survey Team's arrival time. When the message was received and acknowledged by the Takedown Team, the Survey Team was beeped.

Once the message was received approximately 8 targets were taken to the Massport office building. Upon arrival the individuals were met by the Takedown Team at which time the targets were taken off the van, searched and flex-cuffed. Once secured, the targets were taken to the buildings first floor cafeteria that was used as a first-stage booking area. District 7 was contacted and a transport back to the District was scheduled. In all 19 persons were arrested in the takedown phase of the operation with 3 additional people being arrested at their homes by several officers.

Of the 1,105 targeted, 411 letters (37.2 percent) were bad addresses. With regard to the remaining 694 letters, 32 (4.61 percent) responded by calling American Cable. Information from two independent telemarketers proved that a 4.61 percent response rate was well above the industry average of 2.9 percent. Of the 32 respondents, 19 (59.4 percent) went to the staged survey site and were apprehended as a direct result of the operation; an additional 3 people were arrested based on information gathered during the operation. Furthermore, 6 wanted individuals have turned themselves in to the court as of January 12, 1997.

This approach has proved to be an effective alternative to traditional tactics. From approaches such as these we create a lasting impression among those wanted individuals that the Department is relentless in pursuing.

District C-11: Party Line Program

A district wide effort designed to address any type of noise complaint.

In response to the large amount of noise complaints, as well as citizen dissatisfaction in addressing the problem, District 11 developed the Party Line Program. The purpose of this new service was to provide residents with a means, independent of the 9-1-1 system, to address noise complaints. During the planning of the program issues that were examined included: what financial resources were available to find the plan; what would be the most productive time of operation; and how could residents' concerns for a timely and more effective response be addressed.

By allocating money from the Comprehensive Community Grant and Summer Safety Plan, funding, however limited, allowed for the initialization of the program. Hours of operation were based upon a careful analysis of noise related complaints over a one year period. Addressing citizen frustration with the timeliness and manner in which calls were handled was the least difficult to resolve. Through discussions and interviews with residents, and from personal knowledge, the staff of the Community Service Office concluded the responsibility for delays and instances of no response, as well as the perception that officers were often ineffective when they did respond to noise complaints, lay squarely upon call prioritization. Traditionally, officers dispatched to noise complaints will give a warning to those involved to end the activity. If those responsible for the disturbance continue their behavior when the officer leaves it may be some time before another unit is dispatched. In these instances it is unlikely the officer who responds to the call will be available for the repeat complaint.

Upon the examination of the gathered research District 11 developed the Party Line program in July of 1995. Various neighborhood groups and media outlets acted as forums to create community awareness about the program. It was a district wide effort designed to address any type of noise complaint. Three officers and one supervisor were assigned on an overtime basis specifically for this program. There were two shifts in which two officers and a supervisor were assigned to a response unit, while the fourth officer answered and documented calls. All calls for noise complaints were dispatched directly to the unit over channel seven. Shifts were designated from 8:00 P.M. to midnight and 12:01 A.M. to 4:00 A.M. A telephone number assigned to the Community Service Office was created for residents. After a slow start calls became progressively frequent when citizens found that once officers from the Party Line program responded to a complaint the problem ceased immediately. From the beginning of July 1995 through the end of Labor day 1995 (when the program stopped), a total of 271 calls for service had been recorded. In the early summer of 1996, the Community Service Office began receiving inquiries relative to the restart date of the program. By the end of the summer 1996, a total of 435 calls were recorded. This program has provided the citizens of District 11 with an opportunity to address their concerns regarding this quality of life issue.

Index